What people are saying about
From Bethlehem to Baltimore...A Life Journery:

"Clarence W. Hottel, Sr. is a truly Christian man. He has gone about God's work for years. When I was mayor, Mr. Hottel organized our Mayor's {Prayer} Breakfast series and obtained outside speakers. Any works of Mr. Hottel's will be an inspiration not only to teenagers but all of us."

William Donald Schaefer
Comptroller
State of Maryland

"In 1 Timothy 4:12, Paul admonishes young Timothy to be an example of the believer; and I know of no one who more exemplifies that example than Clarence Hottel. For his word is his bond; his conversation, Christ-centered; his charity, agape; his spirit, heavenly inspired; his faith, immutable; and purity, his trademark. I strongly recommend the book and reading about this man, whose life has always been so totally committed to prayer and the glorification of Jesus Christ."

Pat Kelly
Former Baltimore Oriole &
FOUNDER OF LIFE LINE MINISTRIES
Baltimore, Maryland

"Clarence Hottel's book is more than a biography or autobiography; it is truly a monumental story of one man's never-failing faith in God's grace and goodness . . . it is a story with Abrahamic dimensions—a story of faith and sacrifice and a genuine commitment to his Lord and Savior Jesus Christ. Above all, it is a story of a man deeply committed to a life of prayer and the power of transforming life through prayer."

Raymond T. Moreland
Executive Director
MARYLAND BIBLE SOCIETY
Baltimore, Maryland

D0289055

1

"It is an honor to recommend *From Bethlehem to Baltimore . . . A Life Journey.* I have known Clarence Hottel Sr. for many years. His precious testimony, his zeal for the Lord, the impact of his life on our nation's leaders, and his tender care for God's people and work have been tremendously immeasurable. This book captures the chronological history and ministry effort of a life that has been a statesman ambassador for Christ. To Clarence Hottel Sr., the Lord's first words will be "Well done, thou good and faithful servant!"

Richard A. Wilson
Vice President of Stewardship & Advancement
LANCASTER BIBLE COLLEGE
Lancaster, Pennsylvania

"This is a book about personal and spiritual success. If you're looking for flash, razzle-dazzle and celebrity, you've got the wrong book. *From Bethlehem to Baltimore . . . A Life Journey* is how to succeed the old-fashioned way. It's about hard work, integrity and faithfulness in every area of life.

"From Bethlehem to Baltimore . . . A Life Journey is the interesting history of a mom-and-pop company that became a major player in the air conditioning industry. But be careful when you read it. You could miss the point. Because what this book is really about is about one man's deep faith in God and his unspeakable joy in serving his Lord.

Clarence Hottel has what I call quiet greatness. His strength of character, goodness, and Christian grace are an inspiration to all. May his story inspire you to follow in his steps."

J. Thomas Bisset
General Manager
WRBS-FM RADIO
Baltimore, Maryland

"Clarence Hottel is and has been living a Christian life of legendary proportions. He is loved and respected by many as a Christian activist, a successful business-man, and a philanthropist. . . . Here indeed is a model and a challenge for those who sincerely want to 'walk the walk' with Jesus Christ."

Herbert J. Fivehouse
Associate Director for Administration (retired)
NASA GODDARD SPACE FLIGHT CENTER
Baltimore, Maryland

"This book documents the life of Clarence Hottel, my friend. As you read, you will see that he was, and is, a friend of many, both the well known and the unknown, through business and through ministry. You will also discover that Clarence has an intimate friend-ship with God. All of us would do well to embrace the principles he shares in his life's story."

Neil Fichthorn
Former President
SANDY COVE MINISTRIES
North East, Maryland

"This world needs more role models like Clarence Hottel. In his book, Clarence demonstrates the power of a practi-cal, relevant Christianity."

Dr. Kent A. Sutorius
President
MARYLAND BIBLE COLLEGE AND SEMINARY
Baltimore, Maryland

"Whenever I think of Clarence Hottel, I am reminded of the classic description of the Old Testament King, 'As long as he sought the Lord, he was made to prosper.' This is a 20th-century example of a godly industrialist whose life has noteworthy implications and applications for you and me."

Dorwin L. McDonald
Manager (retired)
Industry Affairs
THE TRAVELERS INSURANCE COMPANY
Baltimore, Maryland

"Clarence Hottel provides the reader with a real-world look at the spiritual life and character of a business leader. His example will shine forth for generations to come. A must-read for all businessmen who want their lives to count."

J. Stanley Oakes Jr.
President
INTERNATIONAL LEADERSHIP UNIVERSITY
Empire State Building
New York, New York

"This is a book about leadership in action, the gripping and inspiring life story of a born leader. Clarence Hottel's faith in a powerful God lies at the core of his business practices and his family life, but also shapes his keen interest in what is going on around him here and abroad. The book is filled with fascinating insights into the forces of history over the last seven decades. After all, a 90-year-old with a phenomenal memory for detail looks back on a very rich tapestry of experience and of rigorous stewardship of his resources. Clarence embodies in his actions and prayers what makes America great. You will benefit from this book."

Dr. Freidhelm K. Radandt
President
THE KING'S COLLEGE
New York, New York

"These pages, the life story of my friend Mr. Clarence Hottel, are truly his labor of love for you and all who pause to receive the gift. The apostle Paul wrote to his young friend Timothy with such love and wisdom that Paul's words continue to encourage us today. It is in this spirit that Mr. Hottel shares so freely the joys and sorrows of his life, and shares generously the wisdom of a long and fruitful walk with his God.

"Mr. Hottel brings to his story a special care for men and women who are beginning their life's work. How sad that many of us approach work as little more than an activity that is necessary for paying the bills. Our dreams and faith are too small! Work is God's invitation to join our creative labors with His great labor of creation and redemption. Building on the work of prior generations, we are to bring out ever more intricate features of God's creation and increase the fullness of His kingdom.

"*From Bethlehem to Baltimore . . . A Life Journey* is a true story about God working through the gifts, talents, and obedience of a faithful servant. It is my privilege to recommend this story to all who long to bring their Christian faith into the workplace and the world of business. I pray that the words of my friend will challenge you to dedicate the labor and passion of your life to the greater work of our God."

Dr. David Vader
Chair of the Engineering Department
MESSIAH COLLEGE
Grantham, Pennsylvania

From Bethlehem to Baltimore...
A Life Journey

Clarence W. Hottel, Sr.

as told to Robert C. Larson

FROM BETHLEHEM TO BALTIMORE...A LIFE JOURNEY
Copyright © 2001 by Clarence W. Hottel, Sr.

ISBN 0-9712432-0-4

Printed in the United States of America

Dedicated
in Loving Memory

of my wonderful Father and Mother –
REV. FRANKLIN M. and IDA G. HOTTEL

my Wife and Co-Founder of
Fidelity Engineering Corporation
DOROTHY L. GILLESPIE HOTTEL

our Son
JOHN DOUGLAS HOTTEL
(1941 – 1964)

and in honor of our Children
ANNE, BILL, JIM

and their families

and all
FIDELITY ENGINEERING CORPORATION
EMPLOYEES
Past, Present and Future

During the writing of this book, my dear twin
brother Harvey went home to be with his Lord –
September 2, 1999. These pages are also written in fond
memory of my brother and lifelong pal for 91 years . . .
oh how I miss him!

Table of Contents

- 1908—A Year to Remember
- Let's Go to Church
- Blessed by a Loving Family
- Influenced by the Best
- From Doubt to Faith

- Rabbits, Kites, and Radios
- Wired for Sound
- Then . . . the Crash of 1929
- Lessons Learned
- No Pain . . . No Gain

- A Nation Brought to Its Knees
- "Brother, Can You Spare a Dime?"
- On to Baltimore at Carrier's Recommendation
- America Becomes War-Ready
- Top-Secret Assignment
- How to Win Over Worry

Foreword

Y ou are the same you will be in five years, except for two things, the people you meet and the books you read. Millions have been influenced for good because of the thousands of leaders who have known Clarence Hottel.

The Clarence Hottel biography is a love story. Autobiographies are usually about the person and their achievements. Clarence Hottel's story is about God, Amazing Grace, Blessed Assurance, I Love to Tell the Story, Love Lifted Me, The Wonder of It All, and How Great Thou Art. On every page, in every word you can sense his testimony, "Christ in Me" and "That I May Know Him."

Clarence Hottel in his many years has been a husband, father, businessman, philanthropist, mentor, role model, witness, community leader, but the word that describes him best is servant. Because of his following and yielding to God's leading, he has tasted victories and joy that only a few ever experience. And yet with all his worldly success, he is at home and at ease in whatsoever place or state he finds himself. He knows well that every good thing flows from God and his life story is "All of Grace."

When a man's biography is written, there are three pair of eyes that see it.

1. As he sees it

2. As others see it

3. As God sees it

Carlyle said there is no life story faithfully recorded. He was wrong. The real Clarence Hottel story is recorded in the Book of Life. The ink was the blood of Jesus, the pen was a spear and the parchment was his skin. The Apostle Paul described Clarence's life in Galatians 2:20. *I am crucified with Christ: nevertheless I live; yet not I, but Christ liveth in me; and the life which I now live in the flesh I live by the faith of the Son of God, who loved me and gave himself for me.*

Most men retire at 65 to reward themselves, but not Clarence. He will be giving and serving until the Lord calls him home.

He is the model elder Christian servant. His bags are packed but his tool chest is open. He can confidently say with Paul, "I have fought a good fight, I have finished my course, I have kept the faith; Henceforth there is laid up for me a crown of righteousness" (2 Timothy 4:7-8).

If you know Clarence's Savior, you'll be encouraged and challenged by his life. If you don't know his Savior, the following pages will give you much to think about.

I thank my God upon every remembrance of Clarence Hottel.

Charles E. Jones
President, Executive Books

Acknowledgments

W riting a book about one's life, I've discovered, is a unique challenge. Fortunately, God has given me a good memory (after all, I am on my way to the century mark), reasonable clarity of mind, and a passion for sharing the many gifts my Heavenly Father has given me during a life for which I have no regrets. It will be up to you, the reader, to determine whether I have told my story in a way that brings meaning to your life.

In the process of writing, I quickly became aware of how much a book of this nature must be a "team effort." That is why I feel so indebted to those special men and women who have given me their faithful support, love, and encouragement during these past several months.

To Charlie "Tremendous" Jones, whose Christian testimony has given me great joy for so many years, thank you. You have helped me understand—and keep believing—that everything about life indeed can be *tremendous*.

To Dorothy Drinkwater, my able, trustworthy, and untiring assistant, how can I express my gratitude adequately? Thank you, Dorothy, for your labor of love in doing all you have done to help see this book come to fruition. I could not have accomplished it alone.

To my Southern California-based friend and colleague Robert C. Larson (www.robertclarson.com), who took detailed notes during our many long conversations together, waded through piles of ancient news clippings and old photographs, and with his writing skills crafted them all together in a cohesive manuscript, I say thank you, buddy. I knew you were the right person to do the job the first day I met you. My deepest thanks to you and your beautiful wife, Carolyn, for your professional assistance and personal encouragement.

I would also like to express my thanks to Bob Peterson and his creative team at Back to the Bible, including Rachel Derowitsch, Kim Johnson and Kirk Greuter, for the incredible work each person has done to help make this book a reality. Each person prayed, worked extra hours and endured numerous edits over a period of months—all of which was in a spirit of cooperation and Christian love. Thanks to you all. You're the best!

To my terrific friends at the Carrier organization who helped me complete so many of those unusual low-temperature jobs—never done before—during the United States' preparation for the Second World War, thank you. The interest and guidance from Carrier's top management, along with their ability to obtain and furnish on time the classified equipment we specified and materials needed for the job site, was miraculous. The Carrier manuals and technical data were like a "refrigeration bible."

To my great colleagues and friends at ASHRAE (American Society of Heating, Refrigerating and Air-Conditioning Engineers, Inc.), I can only say this: *it would take an eternity to reveal all the great contributions you have made to help make this world a better place.* You have done wonders worldwide for human beings in the areas of low-temperature refrigeration and air conditioning. What you have accomplished has truly changed the world—for the better. ASHRAE's dedication to the advancement of the art and science of heating, refrigeration, air conditioning, and ventilation, the allied arts and sciences, and related human factors for the benefit of the general public has never wavered. I joined ASHRAE in 1940, was elected treasurer and secretary, and then became president of the Baltimore-Washington, D.C., chapter in 1950, later becoming a life member. These dear ASHRAE friends have encouraged me to write this book, and they look forward to reading about some of the unusual applications of refrigeration they helped us design. Thank you to all my wonderful ASHRAE friends. (See picture on page xvi.)

To my Baltimore Breakfast Group friends, who have urged me to write my life's story for many years, I now say, "Okay, folks, here it is!" Thank you for your love and support during our many years of ministry together. I love you all and thank God for the integrity of your personal lives and your ministry that now spans the world. (See press release on pages 179–182.)

And, of course, to the remarkable staff at Fidelity Engineering Corporation, who have also encouraged me to tell my story for this generation of engineers, and for that group of engineering professionals yet to come. God bless you all. (See page 209 for the 40th Anniversary brochure.)

CWH
July 2001

CLARENCE W. HOTTEL, SR. DOROTHY L. HOTTEL

Co-Founders of Fidelity Engineering Corporation

Reflections

W ho have I become? What will be the conclusion of my story? Only the Good Lord knows how many more years He will add to the 91 I have enjoyed thus far in the journey. What a wonderful feeling to wake up in the morning, thanking the Lord for a good night's sleep. Walking to the bathroom, singing in the shower, I say to myself, Here I am at 91. I can see, I can hear, I can talk, I can walk, I can dress and lace my shoes, and make a good bowl of cereal, and then check and see what is on the calendar for today—not neglecting the prayer list that our prayer group promised to pray for every day. The daily mail, coming from the office and at home, is enough to keep me very busy all day, plus the different places where we have agreed to go to meetings, along with various doctor's appointments I have to keep. I am so blessed, and I am so grateful.

Today is one of those glorious May mornings here in the Pocono Mountains of eastern Pennsylvania. I am relaxed. No tie, no business suit, no phones ringing, no emergencies, no worries about my past, present, or future. Sitting here on the porch of my rustic cottage at Split Rock on Lake Harmony, I feel the early morning chill. My eyes move upward and I see majestic, hundred-foot-high oak trees surrounding "Shepherd Cottage," and those large rocks and huge boulders in the rear. I often wonder who put them there. How can people not believe in God? I ask myself. All this natural beauty could not just happen. Perhaps it is the engineer coming out in me, but if there is a design, must there not be a designer? I am quiet as I eavesdrop on the treetop conversations of some of our local birds, mostly sparrows, robins, northern cardinals and blue jays. I think I can actually hear them echo my sentiments that today is going to be a very special day, filled with limitless promises and possibilities. And over there . . . my faithful friends the squirrels and chipmunks are scavenging for food for themselves and their families.

Shhh. Something suddenly moves in the bushes within a few feet from me and dislodges some piled-up leaves at the side of the porch. To my surprise and delight I see a new baby deer, probably born during the night. Part of me wants to slip over and help the newborn get to its feet. However, I know that would only keep him from doing what he must learn to do by himself. Sure enough—and without my able assistance—my little Bambi pushes one foot out, then another, slipping, struggling, falling to the ground, picking himself up again, finally getting up on all fours with an It's okay, Clarence, I can do this look in his eyes. The deer looks at me, and I look at the deer for the longest time. Then, as if he says, Well, are you going to take my picture, or not? I reach for the camera I always have at my side and snap away as Bambi walks slowly around the back of the cottage looking for mother.

I feel I am at peace with the world. With a friendly book now firmly in hand, some buttered toast, and a cup of steaming coffee, I settle down comfortably and let my lungs take in the fresh mountain air at my oasis perched 2,000 feet above sea level. The air here is different from what we breathe in Baltimore, devoid of carcinogens and omnipresent pollutants. I breathe deeply and it gives me strength.

My life? Well, it is not that complicated, really. Young boy grows up in God-fearing home, sees opportunity, seizes it, struggles with defeat, is endowed with a strong work effort, trusts God, tries to be honest, builds a business, retires, and today feels younger than his years. On occasion I do ask myself, however, how I managed to arrive at the ripe age of 91 and remain in such good health. I confess that I am no longer on the fast track that I enjoyed since age 16, but I imagine I will be forgiven for slowing the pace somewhat. Still, my mind works overtime.

As if by force of habit, I lean back in my chair, turn my head, and look back through the porch window into my living room where I see a picture of my late wife, Dorothy, ornately framed and occupying center stage of an antique end table. My mind floods with memories of how we worked night and day to sow the first delicate seeds that would one day make Fidelity Engineering Corporation a company of integrity and trust. Our overriding goal was to be an honest organization filled with good people who would give our company an unblemished reputation. Service first was always our hallmark, and customer service remains at the heart of our business today. At an hourly rate of pay, my wife and I, together with our sons Bill and Jim, were the lowest paid per-hour employees in our fledgling company. We accepted a minimum wage so we could build up the value and assets of Fidelity Engineering Corporation into valuable shares of stock. We disciplined ourselves to believe that the economic payoff would come later, which it did. We always promised to be good stewards of our money, keep our spending under control, and give a 10 percent tithe to worthy causes.

For the most part, I can say mission accomplished, although I would like to believe there is plenty of life left in Clarence Hottel. I now have the time to relax, although one of my great friends, Charlie "Tremendous" Jones, keeps sending me so many good books that I don't really kick back as much as I thought I might. Instead, I feel compelled to read everything he sends me. I thank the Lord my bills are paid, and that I owe nothing except an enormous debt of appreciation for the friendships I have enjoyed with the hundreds who have given my life such great meaning. Someone once said that God's reward for a job reasonably well done is that He gives him an even bigger job to do. By all accounts, I would imagine I am in that second phase of my life. I enjoy doing my very small part to help feed the poor, bring the gospel to spiritually hungry hearts, and give our nation's youth the opportunity to become the persons God created them to be. Engineering may have been my life, but striving to become God's person has always been my passion.

I remember once reading an author who said his life was a lot like a blue-chip stock: fairly stable, with more ups than downs, and gradually trending over time. Not a bad analogy of my own life. However, when I reflect on the "downs" of the Crash of 1929 and the ensuing Great Depression that created so much havoc in the lives of so many in our country, I must admit that my life did not feel all that "blue-chip." As I sit here reviewing my handwritten notes that describe this terrible era of our history—something I will share with you in subsequent pages—I wonder if it will make you even more grateful for what you have here in the land of the free and the home of the brave: relative security, a stable economy, good working conditions, and the potential for even greater personal accomplishment in the days ahead.

I get up from my comfortable chair and crane my neck, looking through the thick pine branches for my little Bambi. He is nowhere in sight. Perhaps he has already "gotten his legs" and is off scampering with mama and his brothers and sisters who are sequestered among the swaying laurels and nearby waterfalls of the Poconos. I look at my watch, and it is already 11 a.m. Time goes so fast for me these days, even at 91. I suppose that's good. While my mind is still alert, my hearing leaves something to be desired. Yet, the relentless movement of rushing water from a continuously flowing brook has all the rhythm of a great symphony. Hearing loss or not, I pause to listen. I am grateful that in a world of flux some things never change. This sound of water is as soothing to me today as it was the first time I heard it many years ago.

So where am I going with all this? To be honest, I am not entirely sure. I realize the time-honored actuarial charts are no longer in my favor, and that even the "wonders of science" will not help me live forever. So what am I left with? A faith and belief that I am still God's child, that He continues to have a purpose for my life, incidental though it may be, and that as long as I have breath, I will praise and serve the Lord. I may not know the future, but I have ultimate confidence in the One who does. So I now begin to leaf through the copious notes of my life—each page reminding me where I came from, and how, by God's grace, I have arrived at where I am today. Miracle is a word that jumps off many of the pages. Gratitude is another. So I share these musings with you, my reader friend, with the hope that the same God who has always challenged me to do my best work, who showed me the straight path, who gave me a reason for living, and who early on set my feet on a rock, will be the God who can do the same for you.

What greater prayer could I ask for you, and for those you love?

CHAPTER 1

My Childhood

*A perfect example of minority rule
is a baby in the house.*

I wish my father and mother could be looking over my shoulder right now and observe what I am writing. What they would see is an outpouring of love and appreciation for all they did to teach the Hottel children the kinds of values that have been the foundation of our life and work. They blessed us by raising us in a home where parents valued God more than things—even more than their precious children. Sometimes modern parents have difficulty understanding the concept that *children are best loved but not idolized.* We knew we were loved; we also knew that God always came first in our parents' lives. This was never a problem for us. My father, a Mennonite minister, was our spiritual rock: strong, but never harsh; disciplined, but not overly demanding. My parents were persistent in their prayers and in their biblical teaching. When I was born, my father was pastoring three churches in Fleetwood, Blandon, and Terre Hill, Pennsylvania. He and my mother taught us to obey and respect them as they worked to teach their six children— including two sets of twins—to love and respect each other and to give uncompromising reverence to our Heavenly Father. When you are a little kid, it is impossible to know all the challenges your parents are going through. However, when I think of all my dad had to do—and on a young minister's salary—there must have been days when he felt it was a supernatural task.

Twins in coach with ladies from church (1909)

1908—A Year to Remember

I entered the world in the city of Fleetwood, Pennsylvania, on August 6, 1908, along with my identical twin brother, Harvey. As it turned out, we would be very energetic boys with a strong nod toward the mischievous. It was the early years of a new century and a new way of life for millions of Americans. The year before my birth saw the first Model T Ford roll off production lines; more than 15 million would be sold during the next 20 years. The Model T, nicknamed the "flivver" and the "tin lizzie," was probably more responsible for the development of large-scale motoring than was any other car in automotive history. It also spurred the building of roads and streets in the United States. A year later, the General Motors Corporation appeared on the business scene, and the world of transportation changed once more.

Further growth for the country was assured with the completion of the transcontinental railroads—Union Pacific, Southern Pacific, and Santa Fe—and the introduction of the ice- refrigerated boxcar. During the 1908–09 season, 15 million boxes of citrus fruits were shipped east by rail. The fruits were marketed cooperatively through the California Fruit Growers' Exchange, now the Sunkist Fruit Growers' Exchange, whose Sunkist trade name is famous the world over.

In 1908 Theodore Roosevelt called a conference on the conservation of natural resources at the White House. He invited governors, university presidents, businesspersons, and scientists to consider what policy ought to be adopted to preserve the nation's resources for the future. Because of this conference, 41 states created conservation commissions, and the federal government formed a National Conservation Commission.

Joining me on the day of my birth was jurist Thurgood Marshall. Marshall became special counsel for the National Association for the Advancement of Colored People in 1938, and later presented winning arguments before the Supreme Court in many civil rights cases, including the landmark *Brown vs. Board of Education of Topeka* (1954). Marshall served on the Supreme Court from 1967 to 1991, the first African-American to rise to this high judicial appointment.

In 1908 Herbert Hoover, who would be elected president of the United States 20 years later, opened his own engineering firm, with offices in New York City, San Francisco, London, Petrograd, and Paris. The firm served as technical adviser and as reorganizer of failing companies. In the United States, film production was first centered around New York City and Chicago, but the varied scenery, sunny climate, and impressive land of southern California soon attracted film crews. The producers who established the Los Angeles area as a major film center included both independent producers and members of the Motion Picture Patents Company, a trust incorporated by ten companies in 1908. That first decade of the new century turned out to be reasonably eventful, but little did I know at the time just how important it would be.

> **Harvey and I did just about everything together. Even our spiritual lives were in harmony.**

Let's Go to Church

The Mennonite Conference kept my father on the run, sending him from the smallest church in New Jersey to the largest congregations in the Conference in Allentown and Bethlehem, Pennsylvania—some 12 locations in all during his 54 years of pastoral ministry. Through the strong, steady spiritual influence of my father and mother, I invited the Lord Jesus Christ into my life at the age of eight—along with Harvey, my twin brother. As you will read, Harvey and I did just about everything together. Even our spiritual lives were in harmony. It was a moment neither of us will forget. I remember how we cried for joy and prayed with Dad's strong arms wrapped around us. The excitement— even at age eight—of knowing the burden of sin was lifted, that we would one day be with Jesus, and that our names had now been entered in the Lamb's Book of Life was more than we could understand or explain.

My father had an amazing influence on people— especially young people. He knew how to listen, counsel, and love. When he died at 78 years of age, a man walked up to me by the casket and said, "Clarence, I just want you to know I stand here today because of your father. I would not be the person I am today if it were not for his influence on my life. Your dad cared about my problems, my soul. Most important, he cared about me as a person. One day he came to our house when I was a bad kid. He said, 'I'm not going to leave this living room until you make a personal profession of faith in Jesus Christ.' What could I say, except yes! I became a Christian, followed Christ's path, and today I am a Sunday school superintendent in your dad's church."

CHURCH WAS OUR SECOND HOME— OFTEN OUR FIRST.

The Mennonites love to do church, and for us, church was our second home—often our first. We had the usual services on Sunday, of course, but that was not enough. We also had prayer meetings each Tuesday, Wednesday, Thursday, and Friday night. As a leader of one of the prayer services, I learned how to communicate, to listen, and to be responsive to God's calling on my life as I saw Him work through the lives of others.

Dad was working so hard in his three congregations that I often wondered how we could possibly make it financially. Later I discovered how Dad did it. He would appoint a steward to take responsibility for each prayer meeting night, give that person a supply of envelopes for an offering, and then see that the money was allocated to pay the pastor's salary. That is the only way my father got paid—through freewill offerings. If he wanted a pay raise, he had to do only one thing: increase the size of the church. That was the Mennonite way. And that's exactly what he did.

Blessed by a Loving Family

Mother was a model helpmeet for my father. Her specialty was the Sunday school, and through her efforts each church they served over the years grew in numbers and spirit. She loved to go with Dad to visit in people's homes, where she would invite the children to come to Sunday school. Yet with all her church activities, she never neglected her own children. Many nights at three o'clock in the morning I could hear the foot-powered

Mother reading to us in Philadelphia church yard (1918)

Singer sewing machine whirring away as she sat in dimmed light making clothes for her growing family. During the early evening hours, she would take me and my brothers and sisters over to the organ and teach us great hymns and choruses, such as "Yielded" and "My Home, Sweet Home."

I still consider those *Treasury Hymn Books* as among my most prized possessions. Mother made sure Harvey and I took piano lessons at the Conservatory in Philadelphia, a place where we once played a duet at a recital.

Influenced by the Best

Dad seldom ever went out of town without the family, unless it was to attend a committee meeting of ministers from the area. When my father was with us, he was with us. I will never forget the day he took Harvey and me to hear the famous Billy Sunday at his Philadelphia Crusade. What a preacher! He was the firebrand evangelist who shouted statements from the pulpit such as, *When church members stop voting for the saloon, liquor will go to hell. .*

The famous Gypsy Smith would sing and preach to 4,000–5,000 people nightly.

. . The best time for a man to sow his wild oats is between the ages of eighty-five and ninety. . . . Some preachers have to be wet nurses to a lot of 200-pound babies sitting in the pews. His comments on life and the church are legendary. There was nobody like Billy Sunday. Our father would also take us to Ocean Grove to hear the famous Gypsy Smith sing and preach to 4,000–5,000 people nightly. (I still hum many of the well-known crusade hymns that Gypsy Smith taught us that night.)

We loved being with our father, especially when he would take us to Atlantic City. Dad was a strong swimmer and we learned our water skills from him on the beaches of the New Jersey shores. On our way home, Dad always took a side trip to a large peach orchard in the area where we kids would gather huge baskets of fruit. I cannot go into a supermarket today without thinking of those large, juicy, golden Jersey peaches we enjoyed as children.

Everyone knew my father and my father knew everyone—including the owner of a candy and ice cream store on Germantown Avenue near the place where Dad and our church people conducted open-air singing meetings each Saturday night. One day, the candy shop owner took Harvey and me to the back of his store and showed us how chocolate candies were made. The smell of those mounds of chocolate is still in my nostrils. Dad would often surprise us by bringing home several large slabs of chocolate for us to keep cool in our basement—and where we could help ourselves any time we wanted to. How could you help but love a dad like that!

Every summer we spent several weeks on the beautiful Mizpah Grove Camp Grounds.

During my growing-up years life was so good. Every summer we spent several weeks on the beautiful Mizpah Grove Camp Grounds, east of Allentown, where 300–400 tents would house people from 40 to 50 churches throughout eastern Pennsylvania. During the nine years our family was assigned to churches from Philadelphia to Bethlehem, my father served as chairman of the

Dad and tents at Mizpah Grove (East Allentown) camp grounds.

camp meeting for the Bethlehem District. He loved to ring the large bell at church time, a signal for the folks at camp to enter the 4,000-seat auditorium. I can still see (and smell) the dry yellow straw scattered on the floor of the tabernacle, along with the images of happy faces. And I can still hear my father as he led the singing of such hymns as "One Day!" People could not sing the five verses of that song without tears welling up in their eyes.

From Doubt to Faith

As I grew up, I continued to come face-to-face with the temptations any young person encounters. Some days were better than others. Harvey and I had our own lofty business goals and objectives for our successful future. However, we also knew we needed a loving Savior to keep us on track. We saw Christ's love modeled in our parents, but that would not be enough to sustain us throughout life. We knew we must have and maintain a personal relationship with Jesus Christ and live for His honor and praise. Only then would the

35

things of this world grow "strangely dim in the light of His glory and grace." For us, the Bible was the truth, the inerrant Word of God—from Genesis to Revelation. If Harvey and I did not fully understand it, that didn't matter. We were taught to trust and obey it anyway, and to simply accept by faith that which we did not comprehend. I still have the Scofield Bible that my father gave me when I was 16 years of age. I have many Bibles and different translations, but this one, though worn and coming apart, is very precious to me.

It was also at that time when great doubts about my faith and the temptations of life challenged me to make several major decisions on my own—without my parents' permission or direction. Would I deny myself the fun of going along with a non-conforming, anti-God crowd—in direct opposition to all that I had been taught? Or would I serve God and do His bidding? I had to make a choice. Was the Bible true or false? Was its ancient counsel, warnings, and instructions worth following, or would I toss it all aside? I had to make up my own mind—as we all must—and not rely on the spiritual pedigree of others. It is true that God has no grandchildren—only children.

These verses helped Harvey and me make it through the Depression, when we lost everything...

As I ultimately bent toward God and His love, the powerful, instructive words of Scripture took on fresh, new meaning, especially the words in the books of Proverbs and James. Here are two passages from *The Living Bible:*

Every young man who listens to me and obeys my instructions will be given wisdom and good sense. Yes, if you want better insight and discernment, and are searching for them as you would for lost money or hidden treasure, then wisdom will be given you, and knowledge of God himself; you will soon learn the importance of reverence for the Lord and of trusting him. (Proverbs 2:1–5)

"Don't part company with your ideals. They are anchors in a time of storm."

However, what may have been the most encouraging verses were found in James 1:2–5. I have recited these passages for decades, and they remain as fresh today as the first time I read them. These verses helped Harvey and me make it through the Depression, when we lost everything, through the death of one of my children, the terrible loss of my wife, Dorothy, and the uncertainties of business in the modern world. Perhaps these words of comfort will also speak to your heart:

Dear brothers, is your life full of difficulties and temptations? Then be happy, for when the way is rough, your patience has a chance to grow. So let it grow, and don't try to squirm out of your problems. For when your patience is finally in full bloom, then you will be ready for anything, strong in character, full and complete. If you want to know what God wants you to do, ask him, and he will gladly tell you, for he is always ready to give a bountiful supply of wisdom to all who ask him; he will not resent it. (James 1:2–5)

37

Arnold Glasgow once wrote, "Don't part company with your ideals. They are anchors in a time of storm." As I move assertively into my 90s, I say amen to that statement. Ideals. Principles. Integrity. Showing up and working hard. Taking God at His Word. Saying what you mean and meaning what you say: these are the stabilizers that will see you through the challenges of life. Without these as "anchor tenants," the edifice we try to build called business, relationships, and life itself have little chance for survival. With them, however, there is unlimited potential for happiness, fulfillment, and personal growth. This is how I have endeavored to live my life. Even now, I am confident the best is yet to come.

CHAPTER 2

Look Out, Here Come the Hottel Twins

Is your imagination stayed on God or is it starved?
The starvation of the imagination is one of the most
fruitful sources of exhaustion and sapping in a
worker's life. If you have never used your imagination
to put yourself before God, begin to do it now.
—Oswald Chambers

I once heard a story about a little boy who got into a fight with his older brother. Somewhat outmatched, the little guy took quite a beating. It was his pride, however, that suffered most, and the whole terrible experience left him feeling bitter. In fact, he refused to talk to his brother all day. Bedtime came, and their mother, very much wanting to see the two make up, said to the younger, "Don't you think you should forgive your brother before you go to sleep? Remember, the Bible says, 'Do not let the sun go down on your wrath.'" The youngster looked perplexed. He thought for a few moments and then blurted out with a wisdom that can come only from a child, "But, Mommy, how can I keep the sun from going down?" That story sums up much of the life and struggles of the Hottel twins—Clarence and Harvey. We loved each other, but on the way to love we had our share of challenges.

Identical in every way, we drove our teachers crazy. I would pretend I was Harvey, and he would enjoy being Clarence for a day. The hardest part of pulling it all off was just to keep from laughing at the ruckus we were causing. The jokes we played on our friends never seemed to end. If anyone could create a disturbance on the spot, we could do it. The girls we dated were never sure if they were getting what they were promised: Harvey or Clarence. Sometimes they never discovered the truth. Even during our large Hottel family reunion picnics that are held each August, we would hear our relatives say, "Now who is that one again? Harvey or Clarence? I don't

The Hottel twins did just about anything we could to make a few extra dollars.

think I'll ever figure those two out." The more we heard their confusion, the more troublesome we became. We loved it!

The whole scene reminds me of the two brothers who went to their rabbi to settle a long-standing feud. The rabbi, after much persuasion, finally got the two to reconcile their differences and shake hands. As they were about to leave, he asked each one to make a wish for the other in honor of the Jewish New Year. The first brother turned to the other and said, "I wish you what you wish me." At that, the second brother threw up his hands and said, "See, Rabbi, he's starting up again!" Harvey and I may have gone at each other many times, but we would defend each other to the death.

Rabbits, Kites, and Radios

Entrepreneurs from the start, the Hottel twins did just about anything we could to make a few extra dollars. We raised great dogs, specialty breed chickens, and pedigree rabbits, and sold them all for a tidy profit. Over time, we made friends with a local cigar box maker, retrieved the excess long mahogany "strips," and used them to make kites. We saw kite making as a potential gold mine, and before long we had a thriving business selling our handsome, finished products to kids in the neighborhood at the rate of 35 cents a kite—pretty good money at the time.

Father, a dedicated pastor and not an entrepreneur, often thought we should be in the back toolhouse cleaning rabbit pens and not out selling such things as kites. Actually, we continued to do both, and it made us a reasonable amount of money. Our various enterprises taught us at age 13 that a good idea, hard work to implement the idea, and the commitment to keep doing it would eventually pay off.

Our slice of the American dream would be radio...

In that spirit, we kept looking for even better ways to increase our bottom line. So we began to look around. Radio had not yet made its appearance on the national scene. In fact, during the twenties—and even the thirties—it was regarded largely as a plaything. However, we thought radio might conceivably have some business potential, so we decided to learn something about it, just in case it ever got big. During the twenties, the American people, in general, were living comfortably. Business and political leaders spoke of a new era where everyone had the potential for being well off. The American dream was a promise granted to all who were willing to work for it. Our slice of the American dream would be radio, or so we thought at the time.

Still, when our family moved from Philadelphia to Bethlehem, Pennsylvania, radio was virtually unknown, although there were a few scattered stations on the air with limited coverage. Using our wits, a set of simple headphones, some copper wire, and a few crystals, we went into production. At the time there were no radio manufacturers

Harvey and Clarence in 1923 opened their own radio business on the third floor of Laurel Street in Bethlehem, Pennsylvania

such as Atwater Kent, Freed Eiseman, Crosley, Zenith, Grunow, Garod, and General Electric. Anyone who wanted a radio would have to buy all the parts and make it, or buy it from someone who made it for him and knew how to install it to make it work. That's where Harvey and I saw an enormous business opportunity.

Wired for Sound

By the late 1930s, radio had become the miracle of the 20th century as it became possible to hear music and talk through space to people many miles away. Up to that point, this achievement was unrivaled in the history of humanity. But we weren't in the late thirties yet. In 1923 when our family moved to Bethlehem, we knew of no one in that town who could hear a radio broadcast from the few far-away stations available. However, as we put a set of earphones on our potential customers, they marveled at what we had been able to create. Almost everyone who heard a set in operation wanted to buy one. With that, the cash register began to ring. The interest was so strong—and the potential for business so great—that Harvey and I formed Hottel Bros. Radio Sales and Service. We sold sets as fast as we could make them.

Here's how we did it. All the original handmade sets required a properly installed outdoor antenna to get a

clear radio signal. It had to be a straight copper line, 75 to 100 feet long, that was insulated at each

Hottel Brothers In New Store

Enterprising Pair Are Experts in Electrical Appliance Work

Clarence and Harvey Hottel started in business in 1923 in Philadelphia when radio first made its public appeal. They obtained the initial idea of the new venture before the time of manufactures and through experimenting became interested in the field commercially.

Hottel Brothers located in Bethlehem at 520 West Broad street, where they remained eight years until recently when they removed to better and larger quarters at the present location, 520 Main street.

As the radio business developed and the saturation point in radio became effective, the brothers branched out, foreseeing the necessity of other appliances such as refrigerators, radios, electric ranges, washing machines, etc.

They have installed large commercial installations in Lehighton, Easton, Allentown, Catasauqua, Nazareth, Center Valley, Stroudsburg and the Poconos.

Having charge of the Frigidaire service agency for a few years, the brothers branched out, taking over the Copeland distributorship, then Kelvinator, Norge and Grunow. Services on these various makes of machines, makes it possible for them to service all makes of refrigerators as well as radios.

In the radio field Hottel Brothers have had extensive experience with all makes of performance, handling RCA, Atwater Kent, Crosley, Philco, Zenith, now, Armrad, Brunswick, and Electric.

The original Hottel Bros. Radio Sales and Service letterhead.

end and positioned 30–40 feet above ground. As I look back on some of these risky installations, I realize we were in serious danger of falling to our deaths! The first phase of the installation meant we needed to secure a metal band around a high chimney, usually located on a slippery, slanted tile roof. We would attach one end of the antenna to the metal band and connect the other end of the wire to a tree, pole, or another chimney or building. To do this, we used a long extension ladder to obtain the minimum 30-foot height and 100-foot length necessary for good radio reception.

> **God knows we were sincere and willing to do what was necessary to make sure each installation worked and performed as promised...**

God knows we were sincere and willing to do what was necessary to make sure each installation worked and performed as promised, although we certainly risked our lives to secure the mounting of many antennas in difficult places.

However, we were in business. We had taken our chicken, rabbit, and kite endeavors to new heights—literally—and we were determined to be phenomenally successful. Harvey and I will never forget the big neon sign on the roof of a large ice storage building on Broad Street that read ICE NEVER FAILS. Our reaction to that sign (owned by our competitor) was ICE ALWAYS FAILS . . . because it continually melts away. And we thought, Hmmm, perhaps we can do something about that problem someday. And we did!

Then . . . the Crash of 1929

During the 1920s, the Hottel Brothers radio business grew beyond our wildest dreams. However, always the entrepreneurs on the prowl to expand our enterprise, we decided to add appliances and refrigeration to our inventory of products. Soon, we were the main radio and appliance/refrigeration dealer in Bethlehem. The radio business was good and now the appliance/refrigeration side of the store was beginning to pick up.

Business was so good, in fact, that we were able to purchase a double storefront building on Broad Street with two apartments above. The total rent we received covered our mortgage payments. Not only were we teenage business owners, but we were now property owners as

Hottel Brothers store, 520 West Broad Street, Bethlehem

well. We were celebrating our success. Our friends were impressed that we could drive such nice cars—Buicks and Pontiacs—better automobiles, in fact, than our high school teachers were driving.

Shortly after the stock market crash of 1929, however, all our good, paying tenants became victims of the economic disaster and were unable to pay their rent. We had been using their rent money to pay down the mortgage, but without the rent income we were forced to give up the property. Further, Wall Street's panic triggered a general economic collapse, and within a few months many banks began to fail. The Hottel Brothers had been using two such institutions: one for the company and one for personal affairs. We had given the banks our good bonds for collateral against loans we made from time to time. However, when the bonds decreased in value, the bank asked us to make good on our losses, forcing us to pay off the loans with money from our checking account. Before we knew it, the banks' front doors were locked with signs that read CLOSED. The presidents of both banks committed suicide.

Unfortunately, we had sold many of our installations and appliances on a monthly payment installment plan. When Bethlehem Steel Corporation was virtually closed down, leaving thousands of people out of work, our customers could not pay us. Neither Harvey nor I had the heart to repossess their purchases, especially since many of our accounts were good people of our church (where our father was the pastor). We decided to take the losses on honest people who could not pay, collect from those who were able, and do our best to settle with our suppliers. Overnight, the great Hottel Brothers radio and refrigeration enterprise was in business no more. We had learned how to lose—big time. But we never lost our dream.

> We had learned how to lose—big time. But we never lost our dream.

Now older and wiser by the sheer force of personal economic disaster, we had no choice but to close our company, only to be surprised that the Carrier distributor in the Baltimore-Washington, D.C., area offered both of us good jobs. (Dr. Willis H. Carrier, the founder of the company, disclosed his formula and psychometric chart to the industry, and the art and science of air conditioning was born in about 1915.) When my dad learned that I was to be assigned to the Baltimore area, he recommended I have my church membership transferred to Dr. T. Roland Philip's Presbyterian Church, which I did.

My wife, Dorothy, and I made the bold move to a place utterly foreign to us.

It was 1939, and by now I was married. My wife, Dorothy, and I made the bold move to a place utterly foreign to us. We did not know a soul in Baltimore, but we knew of Dr. Philips from his teaching at Percy Crawford's Camp at Pinebrook in the Poconos of Pennsylvania.

Lessons Learned

Throughout the year 2000, I've taken the time quietly to review the many events that have occurred over the past 90-plus years, carefully thinking through the tough lessons I was taught during our first attempts at engaging in business. I suppose the main thing I learned is that "being a Christian" does not absolve one from trouble—or

even a calamity such as the Great Depression.
Being a follower of Jesus does, however, give one
the inner
resolve neces-
sary to push
ahead and to
rise again like
the proverbial
phoenix from
its ashes. It
was during
this period of

"Being a Christian" does not absolve one from trouble...

business disaster that I began to turn to the passage
in James, already quoted in chapter one:

> *Dear brothers, is your life full of difficulties and*
> *temptations? Then be happy. For when the way*
> *is rough, your patience has a chance to grow. So*
> *let it grow, and don't try to squirm out of your*
> *problems.*

I cannot say I didn't try to squirm out of my
problems, but I was confident God was in control
and that He would see me through to a successful
end. Harvey and I learned—or as my dear friend
Charlie "Tremendous" Jones says, "I am learning"—that whenever we faced a brick wall, we were
to rejoice, not complain. We knew we might have
to tunnel through, climb over, dig under, or sneak
around it, but with God's help we were confident
we would get to the other side. Perhaps you can
relate to "hitting the wall." It's no fun. It's messy.
It's often embarrassing. However, there is a reason
for the challenge: it gives our patience a chance to
grow.

Dr. Norman Vincent Peale said it best: "The pressure of modern life against the inner spirit of a

man is great. It is likely to have disastrous results unless we as individuals and as a nation buttress ourselves from within. . . . Faith can give us those inner braces."

No Pain . . . No Gain

The Hottel twins learned this lesson early on—that life is one long series of course corrections, and that there is no direct path to success. I remember when I was 13 how I caused a freak accident at Mizpah Grove Camp Grounds in Allentown, Pennsylvania. Attempting to stop my dad's car as it started to drift from its parking place, I jumped out to get ahead of the moving car as it passed a steel building column. I missed it and was crushed between the steel girder and the car. I could have been killed. When I came to and could breathe, I found myself surrounded by my dad and several other ministers who happened to be nearby. All were on their knees praying for me. Our prayers were answered, thank the Lord. It took about two months to fully recover and get back to normal without any body pain or harm.

As we were passing Aberdeen, a sudden shock of severe pain hit me.

I think it was about July 1940 when early one morning, I was taking a group of our key mechanics to start a rush ventilation and refrigeration job at the Bainbridge Navy Boot Camp Hospital. We stopped and had a good breakfast at the Edgewood

Diner, and then drove on. As we were passing Aberdeen, a sudden shock of severe pain hit me. I pulled off to the side, unable to drive. I noticed the Aberdeen Drug Store across the highway, and I struggled to walk over and tell the pharmacist about my pain. He advised me not to take anything but rather go down the street to a doctor who would examine me and advise me what to do. The doctor looked me over and said he thought it might be a kidney stone. He immediately called the doctor who heads up the genitourinary department at Johns Hopkins and arranged for me to be taken to their Church Home Hospital. Their tests found the stone. With many treatments and hot baths over about a month, the stone was removed without surgery. Thank the Lord! There has been no sign of any kidney stone since.

If I would have had to wait my turn with 10 or 12 people in the doctor's waiting room, I might not have made it..

The year was 1967. In our Ramblewood Road home I woke up one morning with a terrible pain. I came downstairs and told Dorothy and an old friend, Bob Morris, our insurance man, I thought it might be my appendix. As the pain grew steadily worse, Bob offered to take me to his doctor friend where he had an appointment and slip me in his place to have me checked. After I was examined, he called another close-by doctor to double-check and to confirm that it was a leaking appendix. As my pain increased, Bob rushed me to a nearby hospital, Maryland General. If I would have had to wait my turn with 10 or 12 people in the doctor's waiting room, I might not have made it. The doctor's nurse was highly experienced (she may have also been a doctor), and she told me if I had waited another hour, I would not have needed the operation. I always had a feeling that she did the surgery. I was kept in the hospital over a month.

Because I was out a couple of months to regain my strength to full recovery—thank the Lord—our sons Bill and Jim had to take over much of the responsibility of running our company, Fidelity Engineering Corporation. Their duties included the design and quotations for new work, scheduling installations, and directing the installations and service mechanics every day.

My wife's sister, Anamae Gillespie, owned an original rustic cottage at Split Rock on Lake Harmony, Pennsylvania, in the Pocono Mountains. Her many kind invitations and arrangements with the Lodge for our family to come and enjoy her cottage and the Split Rock Resort were greatly

Dorothy and her sister, Anamae Gillespie, who sold us Shepherd Cottage.

appreciated, particularly by our four children and their school friends. After many trips there, with the growing attraction and beauty of the area, we decided to enlarge and remodel Shepherd Cottage, keeping the rustic exterior but making the inside more like a year-round modern home. We also enlarged the picnic area where large groups, or just the family, enjoyed many cookouts.

Anamae suggested to Dorothy that she would be happy to sell the cottage to the Hottel family if we wanted to go forward with plans for enlarging and redesigning the entire interior for modern everyday living, which we did. This included a carport, a new well, a new septic tank, air conditioning, Jacuzzi, and a Jenn-Air electric range and convection oven, equipped with automatic exhaust to prevent smoke and odor inside. We also raised the ground level all around the cottage and provided proper water drainage, including an underground stream tunnel to lead the rush of melting mountain snow and rain to prevent any water in the basement. The top level of the grounds I specified red fine stone instead of grass because Dorothy was concerned about who would be available to keep it trimmed. We had more than 100 evergreen trees planted, which are still growing tall.

> **"I cannot live with this severe pain any longer."**

The contractor hauled large dump truck loads of small red stones and unloaded big piles that had to be raked out smooth and level, which I was doing, enjoying the straining exercise, when all of a sudden I experienced a terrible pain that continued to get worse for the next several days. I finally told Dorothy, "I cannot live with this severe pain any longer." We returned to Baltimore and our family doctor arranged for me to be examined by the chief surgeon on the sixth floor of the Greater Baltimore Medical Center (GBMC), who was Dr. G. Stonesifer, a wonderful doctor. The next day, tests and X-rays pointed to the gall bladder and he recommended surgery the following morning. I remember telling Dr. Stonesifer as I was wheeled into surgery, "I prayed, and with God's help I want you to

> ## AMIDST OUR PAIN, ROMANS 4:21 REMINDS US THAT GOD HAD POWER TO DO WHAT HE HAD PROMISED.

bring me out of this operating room 100 percent perfect and completely relieved of this awful pain, or let me go to glory right from here." He was wonderful. I gave him a Christian book; he read it and wrote me a beautiful letter. This was 1978. Since that day, I have had neither ill effects nor pain. Dr. Stonesifer was a great surgeon with a wonderful personality who cared and kept a close check on me every day with his kind, welcome smile.

Amidst our pain, Romans 4:21 reminds us that God had power to do what He had promised. As the great preacher A. B. Simpson once said, "God is not merely able, but is abundantly able; bountifully and generously able, with an infinite surplus of resources; and eternally able 'to do what he had promised.'" This is the message the Hottel twins tried to live and understand all our days, and the bedrock truth that guided our personal and business lives.

CHAPTER 3

From the Crash to the Bomb

If we are haunted by God, nothing else can get in, no cares, no tribulation, no anxieties ... to be haunted by God is to have an effective barricade against all the onslaughts of the enemy.
—*Oswald Chambers*

W hile the official date for the crash of 1929 was October 24, the economic pain afflicted on millions of Americans lasted well into the early 1940s. It was the worst and longest financial collapse of the modern industrial world—described most aptly as the Great Depression. While today wars, tornadoes, earthquakes, floods, accidents, and terrorist threats capture our attention, these cannot be compared to the profound and all-pervasive nausea of fear and the struggle to survive that accompanied the terrible years of the great economic collapse in our country.

Hysteria and panic swept across America. We found ourselves in the middle of a nightmare from which there seemed to be no recovery. One moment, Americans were living as if there were no tomorrow; the next they were ruled by chaos and confusion. Politicians had spoken of a new era where prosperity would abound. Finally, the American dream would be within the grasp of all. Harvey and I believed it and we took the bait. In fact, we counted on the tidings spoken by the messengers of good cheer. As a couple of kids, the Hottel twins had been successful beyond our wildest imagination. We, too, had bought the line that prosperity was here to stay, but how wrong we were! We received a quick course in Economics 101, and, as a result, our lives were never the same.

A Nation Brought to Its Knees

The Great Depression saw rapid declines in the production and sale of goods and a sudden, severe rise in unemployment. Businesses and banks closed their doors (we knew that from bitter personal experience), people lost their jobs, homes, and savings, and many depended on charity to survive. In 1933, during the worst of the Depression, some 15 million Americans—one-quarter of the nation's workforce—were unemployed. On a personal level, the hardships suffered during the Depression affected many

Employment agency in 1937

Americans' attitudes toward life, work, and their community. Many who survived the chaos of the Depression wanted to protect themselves from ever again going hungry or lacking necessities. Some developed habits of frugality and careful saving; others focused on accumulating material possessions to create a comfortable life, one they promised themselves would be far different from that which they experienced during the Depression years.

Earlier, the self-centered attitudes of the Roaring '20s had fit comfortably with the needs of the economy of the era. Modern industry had the capacity to produce vast quantities of consumer goods, but this created a fundamental problem: prosperity and personal well-being could continue only if demand were stimulated to grow as rapidly as supply. This

> **Physically and psychologically, it was devastating to millions...**

meant that Americans had to be persuaded to abandon such traditional values as saving, postponing pleasures and purchases, and buying only what they needed. The Great Depression had a substantial and varied impact on that idea. Physically and psychologically, it was devastating to millions who not only suffered for lack of adequate food, shelter, and clothing, but who also felt they were to blame for their desperate state. Although few Americans actually died from starvation, many did not have enough to eat. I remember seeing pictures of people searching garbage dumps for food. Many ate grass—some even ate weeds. Malnutrition took its toll on an entire generation. A study conducted in eight American cities revealed that families that had a member working full-time experienced 66 percent less illness than those in which everyone was unemployed.

"Brother, Can You Spare a Dime?"

There had been financial panics in the United States before, and there have been some since, but never did a collapse in the market have such a devastating and long-term effect. Like a runaway roller coaster with its hysterical riders screaming to get off, it gathered momentum and swept away an entire economy before it. The value of money decreased as the demand for goods declined. Statistics, however, cannot tell the story of the extraordinary hardships the masses of people endured. For nearly every unemployed person, there were dependents who needed to be fed and housed. Such massive poverty and hunger had never been known in the United States. Former millionaires stood on street corners trying to sell apples at a nickel apiece. Hundreds of rundown shantytowns—dubbed "Hoovervilles" in honor of the unfortunate Republican president who presided over the debacle—sprang up throughout the country to shelter the homeless. People slept under "Hoover blankets"—old newspapers—to shelter themselves from the elements. People waited in bread lines in every city, hoping for something to eat. In 1931 alone more than 20,000 Americans committed suicide. The theme song of the period became "Brother, Can You Spare a Dime?"

> **IT WAS AGAINST THIS BLEAK BACKDROP THAT HARVEY AND I REENTERED THE BUSINESS WORLD.**

For anyone lucky enough to have a few dimes to spare, Depression America was a shopper's paradise. I remember when a new home could be purchased for less than $3,000. A man's suit cost about $10; a shirt for less than 50 cents. I could buy a pair of shoes for about $4. Milk was 10 cents a quart, a pound of steak only 29 cents, and a loaf of bread a nickel. For a dime we could go to the movies, buy a nickel bag of popcorn, and even have a chance to win prizes given away by the theater. That was for those who had dimes. However, not many of those fortunate enough to be working had much change to spend after paying rent and buying food.

It was against this bleak backdrop that Harvey and I reentered the business world, eager to make our mark. Heads bowed, matured overnight by our steep losses, we knew we had but two choices: throw in the towel as so many were doing, or look for the silver lining within the current crisis and build a business in spite of the economic climate. Years later I would have the privilege of meeting Corrie ten Boom, the Dutch heroine who risked her life protecting Jews during the Second World War in her "hiding place," and who endured the humiliation and pain of a Nazi prison camp where her father and sister Betsie died. Meeting Corrie kindled my interest in the things she

Corrie ten Boom, the Dutch heroine who risked her life protecting Jews during the Second World War.

wrote. When I began to realize what she had endured during the war, I looked back and wondered why I ever complained of the "trauma" Harvey and I experienced during the Depression. These words of Corrie remain firmly planted in my heart:

*I often wonder how it is possible that so many
Christians live like beggars when we are Royal Children, the very children of God. We appropriate one or
two of His promises, but most of them we negate, or
ignore—or reject. If we have been "blessed with all
spiritual blessings in heavenly places with Christ,"
why then do we still so often sigh?*

On to Baltimore at Carrier's Recommendation

For millions of Americans, *sighing* was fast
becoming a national past time. However, Harvey
and I made the decision not to participate. Instead,
we struck out on our own with all the determina-
tion of a couple wild horses: In 1939 Harvey went
to Washington, D.C., and I went to Baltimore, per
Carrier's suggestion. I chose Baltimore because I
believed I could work my way into the fledging
industrial market of low-temperature refrigeration
applications, a field that Carrier wanted covered,
and one I subsequently made my specialty. Had I
not been motivated to do good work, and had I
not maintained a deep relationship with a God
who sustained me through difficult times, Baltimore would have been a lonely place indeed. Even
then, I thought I might not last more than two
years there since Uncle Sam had the temerity to
point his bony finger in my face and say, "Hottel, I
want you!" To help set the stage for the events to
follow, it is important to remember that there were
now sudden demands for low-temperature refrigeration applications to help the United States Air
Forces prepare to win the Second World War
against Hitler's Germany. We were not ready; it
took two years.

On December 7, 1941, the Japanese attacked Pearl Harbor, a deadly raid on our unsuspecting U.S. Pacific fleet that killed more than 2,400 Americans and crippled or destroyed most of the warships and airplanes. The next day, President Roosevelt, with the approval of the United States Congress, declared war on Japan. By this time every patriotic American was willing to do virtually anything to help prepare our country for war. Many started working overtime—often without pay. Every project for the war effort was pushed into high gear as the pressure to prepare a massive attack to stop Hitler increased. Perhaps that is why Uncle Sam figured he needed Clarence Hottel—*to help make the world safer for democracy.* I had already been with Carrier for 24 months in Baltimore, but now that could all change because of the war effort.

One day I went to my mailbox and there it was: a letter that began with

It appeared that I would soon be wearing the uniform of Uncle Sam.

the familiar salutation, "Greetings." It appeared that I would soon be wearing the uniform of Uncle Sam and not one of the Carrier Corporation. Because Carrier felt I had a role to play in the war effort—which would not demand active duty—the manager of the Carrier Air Conditioning Division wrote a spirited letter to my Selective Service Board. I will not reproduce the entire letter here (see page 19-21 for complete text), but these few paragraphs demonstrate what a well-written—and well-placed—piece of correspondence can often accomplish.

Mr. Boucher wrote,

Gentlemen, we are in receipt of a copy of your letter of December 13, 1943, addressed to Mr. Clarence W. Hottel, wherein it is stated that the Appeal Agent has taken exception to Mr. Hottel's temporary re-classification by you as 2A. We appreciate and welcome the invitation, suggested by your letter, to present . . . a resume of Mr. Hottel's experience record such as to qualify him for his present type of activity. It should be recorded that this activity is concerned practically 100% in connection with the war effort.

Permit us to say first and frankly, that we need Mr. Hottel for the functional continuance of our organization. Under the present circumstances we find him not replaceable. . . . Mr. Hottel's total experience in refrigeration activity reaches back sixteen years. Over this period, he has become completely familiar with the personal execution of installation and service work by hand. Thus by his experience, Mr. Hottel is well qualified to conduct and supervise an organization which has for its purpose the design, engineering, installation, maintenance and service of one of the war's vitally essential industries. . . .

Permit us to thank you for your indulgence in connection with the above. We have felt that in bringing these items to your attention, you might incline to agree with our sincere feeling that Mr. Hottel might better be serving his country if left to continue his present work without reservation.

> *Yours very truly,*
> *CARRIER DIVISION*
> *K. D. Boucher*
> *Manager*

Mr. Boucher's letter achieved its stated objective. I continued to serve my country as an employee of Carrier at a time when German submarines were already slipping into nearby Chesapeake Bay, sinking ships carrying the refrigeration equipment that we

> *German submarines were already slipping into nearby Chesapeake Bay, sinking ships carrying the refrigeration equipment that we had shipped...*

had shipped from Baltimore Harbor bound for the ten Air Force bases being built in the Caribbean. For some unspoken reason, these losses were kept secret and we would quietly receive another purchase order to repeat that vessel's shipment. Hitler was doing his best to establish bases in South America, which would give him the relatively easy option of bombing the Panama Canal and U.S. factories.

America Becomes War-Ready

The day after the attack on Pearl Harbor everything changed. Our entire inventory was frozen; every transaction of non-war promotion was canceled. Many Americans suddenly found themselves unemployed and told to get a job in a war plant immediately. America's women slipped on overalls and began working in the nation's factories. This was no time for personal air-conditioned comfort. The country would sweat it out at home so our troops might achieve the military advantage overseas. When it was learned that a theater in Boston was in the process of installing an air conditioning system for comfort cooling, the Freon hit the fan. The Carrier equipment had not yet been installed;

however, our people were already on the job site. The installation was stopped immediately. When one of the war plant's managers in Baltimore heard about the situation, Carrier flew me to Boston to examine the equipment and determine if a complete 50-ton system could be adapted to the munitions factory. It could and it was. I have always hoped that decision helped to save a few American lives.

Two brilliant scientists had just arrived from the atom-smashing project site in Los Alamos...

During the war, many people had come to rely on the superior quality of Carrier technology, developed by Dr. Willis H. Carrier, universally regarded as the inventor of the application of refrigeration. One day, my company received a call from Johns Hopkins University, and I was asked to proceed to the school for a high-level technical discussion. The subject of our meeting was not discussed on the phone. As I approached Remsen Hall, I saw Drs. Burford and Taylor waiting for me. These two brilliant scientists had just arrived from the atom-smashing project site in Los Alamos, New Mexico. They appeared already to have assumed full control over the laboratory and, authorized by the government, they were given top classified clearance. By U.S. government mandate, they had received access to anyone's inventory in the country they might need to complete their project.

When I arrived at the university lab it was ablaze with activity. Everywhere there were testing instruments, dials, wires, vials, glass tubing, and Bunsen burners. I remember feeling that it all had a strong appearance of organized disorder. Dr. Burford took me to the basement beneath the laboratory and showed me a large, custom-made tub lying on the floor. This was where an electrode would be submerged in chemicals to create a hot gas, emitting a strong vapor, which would then be piped up to the laboratory and into a specially designed, heavily insulated cooling tank. The tank, we figured, should probably be mounted high on the mezzanine level so lab workers could drain the strong condensation from those vapors into a hard wax vial from the bottom of the tank. The vapors from the chemicals would be so toxic that the workers would not be able to use metal containers. (They speculated the fumes would be so powerful that they would etch the glass windows along the counter of the laboratory.) The flow of these vapors within the tubing would then be submerged in a calcium chloride brine tank, which had to be maintained at $-100°$ F so the condensing would take place within the tubing at $-80°$ F.

That, in short, is a picture of the intended results of Burford and Taylor's project. We at Carrier were asked to design the tank, determine the amount of insulation needed, and provide professional counsel on where and how to mount it. I knew the labyrinth of the evaporator's coils inside the submerged tank would never be allowed to warm up, and therefore, as a mixture, if they were to leak, there could be a catastrophic explosion. Burford said it could lift the roof off the building. What a terrible thought!

Top-Secret Assignment

After further discussion with the two scientists, and after inspecting the area again carefully, I picked up my two large Carrier manuals and said, "Gentlemen, most of the main items you will need are listed in this manual with a factory printed price list. We will give you a 16 percent government discount if we can count on your authorization to give us an immediate priority work order to proceed on the design and installation." They agreed. I hurried back to my office and quickly put a call in to Syracuse, hoping that I would be able to tell Dr. Carrier himself about this unique application of refrigeration. I knew from being with Dr. Carrier in numerous seminars that this project, whatever it was, would fascinate him greatly. However, he was not available when I called, so I talked to Mr. Logan Lewis, the vice president of Carrier. He said, "Clarence, you know all about Henry Brandt, who is known as the best specialist in low-temperature applications in the country, don't you? Well, he has about 30 calls here waiting for him. However, in the meantime, go ahead and make a sketch with enough information for me to explain it to Henry, and he will call you as soon as he can."

We were simply one corner of a great, clandestine puzzle

None of us knew the details of the project, nor did we think it wise to ask. We simply had a hunch that whatever was going on was somehow vital to our nation's security. We learned later, when everything became public, that this project was one of the world's best-kept secrets. We were simply one corner of a great, clandestine puzzle—each intricate piece coming from a different area of the country—until all could be readied to assemble the final product: *the atomic bomb!* Soon after, Henry Brandt and I, along with our professional engineer, Fred Einbeck, returned to the Hopkins lab to determine where the equipment would be mounted and located. As we had speculated, the large, insulated brine tank would be fitted on the mezzanine high enough for the technicians to drain off the condensation from the bottom of the tank, which was the product everyone was eager to obtain to process and ship by air to a waiting location. (See picture below.)

Clarence Hottel checking the pressure and temperature gauge readings to maintain constant 100 degree below zero refrigeration installation at the John Hopkins Laboratory.

In his first statement to the House of Commons, Prime Minister Winston Churchill promised the people of England something no public relation firm would ever think of suggesting when he said, "I have nothing to offer but blood, toil, tears, and sweat." As our own war machine began to engage the enemy, we also offered these same promises to the American people. For the most part we, too, stood up to the challenge of the oppressor and made ourselves ready for the fight of our lives.

> Living with and for God is the sure antidote for anxiety and despair.

Now, it is more than half a century later, and with the passage of time I ask you two questions: (1) Do we need a real shoot-'em-up war to steel ourselves for the other kinds of battles—infinitely more subtle—that you and I face today? And (2), is it not possible for us to take those same principles for success and cooperation we learned during the war and apply them to how we live in the here and now? Our honest answers will serve as an authentic schematic for how purposefully we are living our lives today. Such honesty before God will also put our hearts at peace and our minds at rest—commodities not all that common in today's world. Living with and for God is the sure antidote for anxiety and despair.

How to Win Over Worry

John Haggai writes in *How to Win Over Worry,* "Mr. Horatio G. Spafford was a successful lawyer in Chicago and a member of the Fullerton Avenue

Presbyterian Church in that city. In the financial crisis of 1873, he lost most of his property. In the stress of the times, he prevailed on his wife and four daughters to take a trip to France—to get as far away from the scene of worry as possible. He booked passage for them on the *Ville de Havre.* They set sail November 15, 1873.

"The trip was uneventful, and its hundreds of passengers were enjoying the indescribable uplift of an ocean voyage. That is, until the night of November 22.

"Shortly after midnight the *Loch Earn,* bound for New York, collided with the *Ville de Havre.* In a few minutes, the French ocean liner sank beneath the waves. The *Loch Earn,* which was not damaged by the collision, rescued as many survivors as they could find. Of the 226 passengers on the *Ville de Havre,* only 87 survived.

'Saved alone. Children lost. What shall I do?'

"Mrs. Spafford was among the survivors, but the four daughters perished. As soon as Mrs. Spafford reached land, she telegraphed from France to her husband, 'Saved alone. Children lost. What shall I do?'

"The Chicago attorney left immediately to join his wife and bring her back to Chicago. It was in the depths of their bereavement that he wrote his one and only hymn, 'It Is Well With My Soul.' The grief of his terrible loss and the peace he experienced as he and his wife submitted their lives to God's providential dealings, he describes in the four stanzas of the hymn.

"Perhaps the words will take on new meaning for you as you ponder them:

When peace like a river attendeth my way,
When sorrows like sea billows roll,
Whatever my lot,
Thou hast taught me to say,
'It is well, it is well with my soul.'

Though Satan should buffet, though trials should come,
Let this blest assurance control,
That Christ has regarded my helpless estate,
And hath shed His own blood for my soul.

My sin—oh, the bliss of this glorious thought—
My sin, not in part but the whole,
Is nailed to His cross and I bear it no more!
Praise the Lord, praise the Lord, O my soul!

And, Lord, haste the day when the faith shall be sight,
The clouds be rolled back as a scroll,
The trump shall resound, and the Lord shall descend!
Even so—it is well with my soul!

"Christian friend, before you were saved you had no peace, did you? The Christless heart is like a troubled sea that cannot rest. There is no peace for it.

"Now that you are a Christian, the Lord has brought you peace with respect to your relationship with Himself and with respect to your outlook on eternity. However, if you are to enjoy the peace of God over daily worries and cares and anxieties, small though they be—'the little foxes spoil the vines'—we must fix our mind upon Him. 'Looking unto Jesus' (Hebrews 12:2).

"Keep your mind 'stayed' on Him. This will enable you to fulfill the Bible formula of Praise, Poise, and Prayer.

"Here is the glorious conclusion:

Praise plus Poise plus Prayer equals Perfect Peace!

"As Christ lives in you, 'your peace shall be as a river, and your righteousness as the waves of the sea.'

"Peace be with you!" [1]

And, I would add my own favorite chorus to the one cited in this moving story, inspirational words I learned from the dedicated lips of the great preacher Gypsy Smith so many years ago:

Oh, to reflect His grace,
Causing the world to see,
Love that will glow
Till others shall know
Jesus, revealed in me.

The message of this chorus has been my lifelong desire—to reflect the love and grace of my Savior, and to be the kind of example to others that will bring glory to His name. Two other hymns that have given me such great joy and sustenance throughout my life are J. Wilbur Chapman's "One Day!" and "He Giveth More Grace," by Annie J. Flint. It is my prayer that the words of these great songs of the faith will touch your heart as they continue to touch mine.

---

[1] John Haggai, *How to Win Over Worry*. Harvest House Publishers (Eugene, Oreg.: 1959, 1976, 1987), pp. 195–197.

One Day!

One day when heaven was filled with His praises,
One day when sin was as black as could be,
Jesus came forth to be born of a Virgin,
Dwelt among men, my example is He!

One day the trumpet will sound for His coming,
One day the skies with His glory will shine;
Wonderful day, my beloved ones bringing;
Glorious Saviour, this Jesus is mine!

Living, He loved me; dying, He saved me;
Buried, He carried my sins far away;
Rising, He justified freely forever:
One day He's coming—oh, glorious day!

He Giveth More Grace

He giveth more grace when the burden grows greater;
He sendeth more strength when the labors increase,
To added affliction He addeth His mercy;
To multiplied trials, His multiplied peace.

When we have exhausted our store of endurance,
When our strength has failed ere the day is half done,
When we reach the end of our hoarded resources,
Our Father's full giving is only begun.

His love has no limit; His grace has no measure;
His power has no boundary known unto men.
For out of His infinite riches in Jesus,
He giveth, and giveth, and giveth again!

During these many decades on planet Earth—
from the crash, to the bomb, to engineering business success, and to what is still a bright future
indeed—my Lord has never let me down, never disappointed me, and has always stuck close by during
my every need. Praise God for His great love!

CARRIER AIR CONDITIONING DIVISION

OF

United Clay and Supply Corporation

1122 N. CHARLES STREET
Baltimore, Md.

December 21, 1943

Selective Service System
Local Board No.11
428 York Road
Baltimore 12, Maryland

Subject: Clarence W. Hottel, Order No. 1576

Gentlemen:

We are in receipt of a copy of your letter of December 13, 1943, addressed to Mr. Clarence W. Hottel, wherein it is stated that the Appeal Agent has taken exception to Mr. Hottel's temporary reclassification by you as 2A.

We appreciate and welcome the invitation, suggested by your letter, to present, for the consideration of the Appeal Board, a resume of Mr. Hottel's experience record such as to qualify him for his present type of activity. It should be recorded that this activity is concerned practically 100% in connection with the war effort.

Permit us to say first and frankly, that we need Mr. Hottel for the functional continuance of our organization. Under the present circumstances we find him not replaceable. Qualified by his experience record he has been employed as a skilled managing executive of the Carrier Division of our Baltimore operation since coming with our Company two years ago. Prior to that time he was associated with the former Carrier Distribution outlet in this area, as Manager of the Commercial Refrigeration section. This latter association covered the period from 1937 to 1941.

Mr. Hottel's total experience in refrigeration activity reaches back sixteen years. Over this period he has become completely familiar with the personal execution of installation and service work by hand. Thus by his experience, Mr. Hottel is well qualified to conduct and supervise an organization which has for its purpose the design, engineering, installation, maintenance and service of one of the war's vitally essential industries.

Mr. Hottel's acceptance by the Refrigeration Industry, in turn, needs no further qualification. It is a matter of record that he and his work are accepted.

CARRIER AIR CONDITIONING DIVISION

OF

United Clay and Supply Corporation

1122 N. CHARLES STREET

Baltimore, Md.

December 21, 1943

Page 2.

It may interest the Board to recall the fact that Mr. Hottel last year, delivered before the combined Baltimore and Washington sections of the American Society of Refrigeration Engineers, of which he is a member, a highly instructive and well received dissertation covering the "Highway Transport of Refrigerated Foods". The problem reflected by the above title is of considerable importance towards our Army's successful continuance of the war.

We dare say further that Mr. Hottel's personality is well known to practically everyone in the northeastern area of our country, connected wholly or in part, with the Refrigeration Industry. These facts may readily be checked.

We acknowledge Mr. Hottel to be:

A. A specialist in problems of food storage, freezing, preservation and transport.

B. Thoroughly familiar with the mechanics of low temperature refrigeration, - to temperatures reaching approximately minus 100° F.

C. In full command of the thermodynamics involved in applications involving constancy of temperature and humidity.

D. A specialist in problems of heat exchange.

These qualifications are presently finding expression in the following installations.

A. Refrigeration for hydrogen-fluoride condensing at minus 75°F at Johns Hopkins University - Governmental Research.

B. Constant temperature and water cooling application on Mobile Ballistics Trailers, "Slave Stations", for Aberdeen Proving Grounds.

C. Constant temperature and constant humidity application for Gassing Chamber being erected for Edgewood Arsenal.

D. Refrigeration involved in rehabilitation of existing storage refrigerators at Camp Meade.

CARRIER AIR CONDITIONING DIVISION

OF

United Clay and Supply Corporation

1122 N. CHARLES STREET
Baltimore, Md.

December 21, 1943

Page 3.

E. Dehumidification of underground storage facilities at Fort Miles, Lewes, Delaware.

F. Chilling and storage at minus 10° F of Bulk Alloy Metals for Glenn L. Martin Company, Baltimore.

G. Constant temperature and humidity application at Mt. Vernon-Woodbury Mills, - Textile Research.

H. Heat exchange applications at Pittsburgh Plate Glass Co., Baltimore - in connection with synthetic bristle production.

I. Constant temperature and humidity application for Julian P. Friez, Baltimore, - Research Laboratory (plus or minus one-tenth of a degree)

J. Constant temperature and humidity application in explosive mixing and packing enclosures at Porcelain and Enamel Manufacturing Company, Baltimore.

K. Refrigeration service, general - at Bainbridge Naval Training Station, Port Deposit, Maryland.

L. Industrial heating and dehumidification of Plating Room at Koppers Co., American Hammered Piston Ring Division, Baltimore.

M. Forty (40) installations, - general refrigeration, - at Naval Stations throughout the Caribbean Sea area.

N. Constant temperature applications at the laboratories of Hynson, Westcott and Dunning, Baltimore, - sulfanilamide and penicillin production.

O. Maintenance of dehumidification equipment in Baltimore City Water Pumping Stations.

P. Radar laboratory at the United States Naval Academy, Annapolis, Maryland.

Q. Telephone Exchange Building installations at Aberdeen, Edgewood, and Camp Meade.

CARRIER AIR CONDITIONING DIVISION

OF

United Clay and Supply Corporation

1122 N. CHARLES STREET
Baltimore, Md.

December 21, 1943

Page 4.

R. Western Electric Company dehumidification application
for Cable Dehydration.

S. Storage refrigeration at plus 10°F., Camp Holabird.

Besides essential work involved in the engineering and
installation of the above, it should be noted that Mr. Hottel's
activity includes the direction and follow-up involved in the sup-
ervision of maintenance and service. In other words, to a large
extent, it is his responsibility to keep this equipment running in
order to provide the proper humidity and temperature conditions required in these industrial plants to keep up production.

Permit us to thank you for your indulgence in connection
with the above. We have felt that in bringing these items to your
attention, you might incline to agree with our sincere feeling that
Mr. Hottel might better be serving his country if left to continue
his present work without reservation.

Should you feel that further elaboration is necessary,
perhaps better by personal interview, please let us know.

Yours very truly,

CARRIER DIVISION

K. D. BOUCHER
MANAGER

CHAPTER 4

Sweating Out the War

The greatest success is not in never falling,
but rising each time you fall.
—Vince Lombardi

W hen Thomas Edison and his assistants had finished an improved prototype of the first electric light bulb, the great inventor handed the bulb to a young helper. As the boy nervously carried the fragile bulb up the stairs, it slipped from his hands and fell to the ground, smashed into tiny pieces. Undaunted by the mishap, Edison put in the long, extra hours needed to produce yet another bulb. When he was finished, he handed it to the boy who had dropped the first one. I am sure you can imagine the terror that rose in the lad's heart. Yet, in that simple gesture of confidence, Edison may have changed the boy's self-image from one of failure and incompetence to one of success and confidence. Rather than let his young worker wallow in a mistake, by giving him another chance Edison taught the boy that he could rise above his failure.

I think of that story often as it relates to my early work with Carrier in Baltimore. Repeatedly the people in charge of our division gave me opportunity after opportunity. They believed in me and, as a result, I was able to develop greater confidence in myself. Here's my point: being unable to rise above failure can prevent you from getting up when you have been knocked down. However, failure itself can also be a tremendous learning experience. *That's why I encourage you to view whatever mistakes you make today as valuable teachers. Instead of saying, I am no good, or, I really blew it this time, ask your-*

Failure itself can also be a tremendous learning experience.

self, What can I learn from this situation? How can I use this challenging experience as an opportunity for growth? I asked myself these questions many times during my early years as a refrigeration engineer. I am still asking them today, even in my 90s, and will probably continue my quest for self-improvement until the day I die.

The Phone Keeps Ringing

During my early years with Carrier, we had many highly sensitive operations going on simultaneously, which means we received scores of telephone calls from existing and new clients on a regular basis. However, our participation in the project that would ultimately produce the atomic bomb quickly rose to the top of our list of priorities, largely because of the pressures the government placed on authorized companies to give up their materials. If we needed a plate of copper from someone's inventory anywhere in the country to fabricate a condenser, it was immediately shipped to Carrier so we could integrate it into a product. It was the same with condenser and evaporator coils. Whatever we needed, we received.

For the interest of the many refrigeration engineers who will read this book, here is a partial list of the kinds of calls we at Carrier received, and the types of applications that were required.

• An unusual historic request came to us for constant dehumidification of the underground storage facilities at Camp Miles, Lewes, Delaware, where large guns and powder were stored secretly underground, ready for immediate use to defend our eastern shore against enemy attacks. (The entire upper area of the facility was covered by a grass lawn, thus preventing it from being seen from the air.) To meet the requirement of the assignment, we decided to use two three-ton, air-cooled compressors mounted on heavy planks of a self-contained package, ready to plug into a generator or other source of power. We set the controls to maintain

Army engineers were building a special chamber where they would test "gassing soldiers."

approximately 40º F *leaving the evaporator coils* and approximately 125° F *leaving the condenser coils*. With this mixture we discovered we could maintain approximately 45–60 percent relative humidity in the underground storage area, which satisfied Army engineers. I believe the "watching posts" around the Rehobeth Beach area are still in place today.

• An assignment from Edgewood Arsenal indicated that Army engineers were building a special chamber where they would test "gassing soldiers" (who offered to be tested) along with horses—with special built-in controls that would permit us to control the gases, temperature, and humidity to determine their reaction on both hot and cold days at different humidities.

• Another important call came from the Glenn L. Martin Company in Baltimore asking us to install a refrigeration system that would maintain 10º F for their bulk storage and alloy metals.

• The Mount Vernon Woodbury Mills Company in Baltimore, which manufactured heavy ropes for Navy ships, also made inquiries of Carrier. Its primary sources of material supply had been restricted and the company was operating a textile research lab, which required a constant temperature- and humidity-control system. Carrier designed and installed the system.

> **A special research laboratory wanted to know if Carrier could furnish and install refrigeration equipment to hold the enclosed area of its lab at a plus or minus one-tenth of a degree.**

• A most unusual call came in from Pittsburgh Plate Glass Company in Baltimore asking us to help design a method of chilling its synthetic bristles for the manufacture of paintbrushes. The company's source of bristles from pigs had been cut off by the war. We worked out a procedure where the roll of long, thin, black strings of synthetic material emerged from the machine and moved directly into a long metal trough filled with 34º F water. This near-freezing temperature caused the strings to harden as they flowed to the end of the long trough. They were then dried and prepared to be cut into bristles for binding on to paintbrushes.

• I vividly recall receiving a call from the Julian
P. Friese Company of Baltimore, a control manufacturer, whose special research laboratory wanted to
know if Carrier could furnish and install refrigeration equipment to hold the enclosed area of its lab
at a plus or minus one-tenth of a degree. We were
finally able to hold the temperature at that
extremely close condition by determining the exact
constant heat load and then changing the variable
speed of the compressor several times to match. We
calculated the precise displacement capacity of the
compressor without allowing it to short cycle or
turn off and on, which would have shown a dip in
the recording. This installation was considered a
rare application at the time, but with persistent
resetting and adjustment of the operation the system met the specified conditions.

• On one occasion we received a War Production
Board authorization to repair and recondition the
breakdown of old refrigeration for dehumidification systems in the Baltimore City underground
water pumping stations, which would assure our
city of uninterrupted water supply for our war
plants.

• The United States Naval Academy in Annapolis,
Maryland, authorized Carrier to design and install a
humidity- and temperature-control system for its
radar laboratory. Installation was promptly accomplished.

• The Army authorized us to design and install
dehumidification and air-filtering installations in
three telephone exchange buildings in Aberdeen,
Edgewood, and Camp Meade, Maryland. The system would allow personnel there to close the win-

dows and doors and thus eliminate the dust and moisture on the thousands of delicate contact points and controls.

• There was an emergency call from the Western Electric Company authorizing us to work on a refrigeration application for cable dehydration. When completed, the system removed moisture during high-humidity days in the "rush production" area. We also designed a system to remove the terrible cloud of lampblack dust that was polluting the air.

> *We were not told what would be stored in this room. To this day I do not know the reason for our installation...*

• We received an urgent call from the Army to install a refrigerated storage room to maintain plus 10º F at Camp Holabird. We were not told what would be stored in this room. To this day I do not know the reason for our installation, which was authorized by the War Production Board.

• At Bainbridge Training Station, Port Deposit, Maryland, we were called upon to install different kinds of refrigeration in the base hospital. In addition, we were asked to design a large icemaker that would produce some 300–500 pounds of ice per day—enough to meet the thirsty demands of more than 50,000 boot camp trainees. We also designed and installed pre-fab, sectional walk-in coolers.

• Another project I developed at Bainbridge would allow several hundred young men to crowd into the telephone building after dinner where there were hundreds of pay stations. The soldiers would stand in line and smoke until the air was so blue with fumes that I could hardly see, much less breathe. The telephone company called us to put our people on overtime to install a ventilation system to remedy the problem, which we did. (I often wonder how many lives could have been saved had there been the smoking awareness programs that exist in our country today.)

• Some calls Carrier received were important but not urgent. Others demanded our immediate attention. I remember one emergency order that came from the Porcelain Enamel Manufacturing Company in Baltimore that asked us to survey, design, and install a guaranteed, constant-temperature humidity system at its plant. Originally a leading manufacturer of porcelain casings for appliances such as washers, dryers, tubs, and Frigidaire refrigerators, the facility was now being converted into a war plant. When we arrived at the entrance to the plant, we were greeted with the instructions that there would be no smoking. They then checked us to insure that nothing on our persons could cause a spark that might ignite the explosive powder they were mixing from a giant mixer and sealing in small drums. The hot weather and lowering dry humidity created an immediate need for humidification and cooling. We wore moccasins to cover our shoes for fear the nails in our soles might cause a spark. We walked gingerly around the plant throughout the day. Without this application there was fear of an imminent explosion. While we were

> **Without this application there was fear of an imminent explosion.**

still trying to determine the end use of the powder, one of the company's people informed us that it would be used to create a great smoke cloud so enemy planes overhead could not see when our troops were about to invade.

God, Country, and Creative Engineering

Another call came from Edgewood Arsenal, where a construction contractor was required to provide temperature and humidity control for several rooms that had the appearance of a miniature hospital where animals (mostly dogs) were used to test different types of projectiles. The projectile being tested would penetrate the leg of a dog under high-powered X-ray. The slowed-down picture of the X-ray showed what happened as the bullet penetrated and if it shattered or spread. The dog would then be taken immediately to the adjoining emergency room and cared for by doctors who also ran tests, repaired the wounds, and thus saved the animal's life. Our installation provided the climate control for the personnel at Edgewood Arsenal to do its wartime assessments. While it is controversial to use animals in lab testing today, such procedures were justified 50 to 60 years ago because of the need for immediate, critical information that would contribute to the war effort. While some animals suffered, countless American lives were saved.

The Company's Private Effort to Help Topple Hitler

Whenever the telephone rang, we never knew how our team's talents would be tested next (these war-time projects were done while I was still employed with Carrier). Still, we were always ready to spec out a job and respond to any reasonable assignment—and some that were probably not so reasonable. One day I picked up the phone and it was a call from Koppers Company, the American Hammord Piston Ring Division. The company wanted us to survey and arrange for the installation of an industrial heat and dehumidification system that would provide accurate temperature controls for its plating room. Of course, even as our customers do today, they wanted it *done as soon as possible.* Some things in life never seem to change! The company was losing approximately 20 percent of its cast-iron piston ring production as rejects because of the constant temperature changes and varying high humidity. There was good reason they wanted their problem fixed *now.*

> *We felt we were making one contribution after another to the war effort and to the ultimate defeat of Hitler...*

At the time of our negotiations with the leadership at the factory, a pitched battle was already being fought in the desert sands of Africa. Hitler's top general, Rommel, the German field marshal known as the "Desert Fox" for his North African triumphs, was commanding the troops assigned to repel the expected Allied invasion of France. As one might expect, to fight in the austere conditions of the desert with modern equipment had its own unique challenges—one in particular: General Montgomery's Allied planes and tanks stirring up so much sand, dirt, and grime that the rings in the engines of our war machines had to be replaced repeatedly, greatly increasing the need for their replacement—too often, we were told. It was our job to meet this challenge where the problem began: *in the factory where the rings were produced.* Again, as it happened so often, with great pride we felt we were making one contribution after another to the war effort and to the ultimate defeat of Hitler and his intolerable Third Reich.

Teamwork Helps Win the War

I remember the growing tension that was building as Hitler's battle-hardened force of seven million soldiers swallowed one small European nation after another, with the ever-present reality that he would one day land on American shores. Hitler was no imagined threat. He was real! The only way we kept the madman and his Third Reich at bay was by sticking together as a people and working longer hours and harder than we had ever worked before.

U.S. infantry wade to Omaha Beach, Normandy, France under heavy German fire on D-Day, June 6, 1944.

I cannot verify it, but I have a hunch that the powder we helped to design as a smoke screen against enemy fire may have been used in the Normandy invasion (D day). On June 5, 1944, planes carrying 24,000 paratroopers set off from England. The next morning, some 5,000 vessels of every kind landed an attack force of more than 130,000 soldiers. Ten thousand casualties resulted from the assault, but the tide was turning in the Allies' favor.

I want our younger generation to know how important it was to work as a team during the war and that it is equally important to work together in harmony during peacetime. Neither war nor business is a one-person arrangement. No one individual can know it all. Only when we work together will we discover our own personal skills and gifts. That is how it was during the war. There was tremendous pressure to produce quality materials for the war effort, and at a higher rate of speed than had ever been demanded of us in the past. Some days we wondered what the war's outcome would be.

Sir Winston Churchill, 1945

Even as we questioned the future, one figure would continue to emerge who gave hope to the entire free world, a man who deserves much of the credit for victory. He was a paunchy, cigar-smoking, unimpressive-looking man who held his country together by stern, no-nonsense words and uncompromising actions. While other voices shouted "Surrender!" Sir Winston Churchill would champ on his cigar, put on his war face, and dig in his heels more firmly. In London, bombs devastated city block after city block; massive buildings crumbled, sturdy bridges collapsed, but the stubborn Prime Minister refused to budge. Never once did he default to negotiations. Instead, he operated on a simple rule of thumb when it came to winning a war. Wars are not won by evacuations.

I would encourage you to take some time to read and reflect on Churchill's many books and speeches. It is an excellent method of studying modern history, and perhaps the best way to become intimately acquainted with one of our world's greatest leaders.

The Work Never Ends

I learned one thing quickly: business is not the same during war as it is in peacetime. In war there are no excuses for delays. Since the only cry we ever heard from the government was *How fast can you deliver?* we were able to obtain contract after contract with almost no mention of cost. Everyone everywhere was working overtime. Factories that once produced domestic goods became war plants working three shifts per day. I felt the same pressures as I was asked to promise that I would order the equipment by telegram that very night, even if it took me until five o'clock in the morning to summarize the details on my purchase orders—which often happened. Later, I discovered those government agencies with higher priority would demand that a Navy or Army lieutenant appear at a factory to expedite an order to our job site for immediate installation.

It is still as clear as if it were yesterday. The call came early in 1941. I was instructed to go to the top floor of the American Building on Calvert Street in downtown Baltimore as quickly as possible. Upon arrival, I was escorted into a room frantic with activity where I was questioned about two things: my government classified clearance, and my qualifications regarding the design and application of Carrier refrigeration equipment. I was then introduced to the presidents of three of the largest general contractors in the East: Consolidated Engineering in Baltimore, Hardaway Construction, from Virginia, and the Arundel Corporation. Everyone in the room was either standing around or talking on the telephone. I was asked to sit down next to an architect who was making sketches from the information he was receiving from a full-dressed Navy officer. The officer was on the telephone talking to construction management in the Caribbean Islands, where the Navy was preparing to construct a building to house groups of construction workers. They also wanted a Navy section in each one of the ten Air Force bases in the region.

Poster encouraging skilled workers to enlist in 1941.

Initially, I thought they were talking about only *one* Air Force base, and I began to complete my paperwork accordingly. When one of the contractors interrupted me and said it was *ten* not *one*, I almost fell off my chair. When I gained my composure, I asked, "Do you mean you want ten times this one complete assembly for approximately 300 people in each Air Force base?" Without a smile he said, "Yes. That's exactly what we want." I quickly crossed out the "one" and changed it to "ten." I was glad I had brought my factory manuals, along with the data necessary to show them pictures of the type of equipment that would be required, how much space would be needed, and the amount of electrical power necessary for the kitchen and walk-in coolers. I was glad I had recently redesigned the air conditioning and refrigeration at the famous Miller Brothers Restaurant in Baltimore, which could accommodate between 200 and 300 people. That job gave me an immediate idea how much equipment and space would be needed for the different foods and items that modern restaurants might require.

> *The only difference now was that I would be involved in a project that would ultimately save American lives.*

I think the Navy may have been surprised that I had so much of this data on the tip of my tongue. It wasn't any genius on my part. I had just completed a similar assignment and the information was close at hand. The only difference now was that I would be involved in a project that would ultimately save American lives. The new job for the government was much more challenging—and fulfilling—than doing the refrigeration redesign of a restaurant.

As I was listing the items that would be needed on each of the ten Caribbean bases, one of the contractors standing over me asked if I knew the president of the company I was representing for this particular project. I said, "Yes, I do." He asked me, "What's his name?" I said, "It's Jerry Tyler, president of Tyler Fixture Corporation." He ordered his secretary to get him on the telephone. When he finally connected with Mr. Tyler, the contractor asked why I had recommended an extra inch of insulation—from a three-inch to a four-inch thickness. I had already told him the extra inch of thickness was needed because of the excessive heat in those islands. Further, he questioned why I had suggested it be installed in a special type of box. The contractor had objected to my specifications, saying that it would take more time than was necessary. *After all, Mr. Hottel, there's a war going on.* Jerry Tyler said, "I'll call you back in ten minutes." When he returned the call he said, "Mr. Hottel is right. We checked the average temperature in that part of the world and it would be best if you went with the four-inch insulation." They would have rather accepted the standard three-inch insulation to get delivery much quicker, but it would not have been a wise decision.

> *All the reading and research in the world cannot compensate for what we can learn in Holy Scriptures.*

This rush order totaled 40 refrigeration assemblies to the ten bases on different islands. It was a good—and hectic—business day! I stayed up all night to telegram the factories our top-priority orders to rush the shipments to the different islands of the Caribbean, as specified.

Steps of Faith

Sometimes we may think that business is business and that nothing spiritual could possibly have any bearing on our chosen enterprise—that there must be a wall of separation between the world of the true believer in God and His Church, and the world of business, the marketplace. My experience of many years suggests the opposite. Both require a firm step of faith founded on four principles. Permit me the following reflections:

1. The inspiration and counsel found in the *daily reading of the Word of God* gives us our energy source for living. All the reading and research in the world cannot compensate for what we can learn in Holy Scriptures.

2. For a refrigeration specialist like myself, I discovered the *importance of having my data manuals with me at all times.* They provided me with sound, constant engineering support— both on-site and when writing proposals for a project. This was particularly important for me because of my active role in ASHRAE (American Society of Heating, Refrigerating and Air-Conditioning Engineers, Inc.).

3. I always had Carrier application manuals with equipment specifications and installation pictures in my possession. The Chinese are right: *a picture is worth a thousand words.* Many sales have been lost or hopelessly delayed because this information was not readily available.

4. I always asked suppliers of equipment to guarantee their quotations in writing, to produce detailed specifications, and to provide factory-printed prices and discounts. This was for the protection of all parties involved. It was a good practice then and it remains good business today.

These four aspects of my spiritual and business life have been the fulcrum on which I have stood since my earliest days with Carrier and in the many years of service with my own company, Fidelity Engineering Corporation. Throughout the years, I have learned it was important to know all about what I was selling, to follow through to the completion of the project, and to have the owner/customer sign our completion slip, with a copy sent to the office for billing, including any extras—indication that the installation was performed as promised in the proposal contract.

> ## "He can turn it into gold if we trust Him to turn adversity into your own advantage."

We all know the feeling of exhilaration when all is going well: when we get the job, do the work, send the invoice, and the client pays. However, as my good friend Bob Cook used to say on his daily morning radio broadcasts, "You never know when you pick up the phone or open the morning mail whether it will be a shock and a sting of disappointment, or good news that will brighten your whole day." But even if the news is bad, and even if there seems to be more tribulation than joy, I hope that together we will remember what Dr. James Kennedy often reminds me, "In the midst of heartache, disappointment, and pain, God can do the unimaginable. He can turn it into gold if we trust Him to turn adversity into your own advantage." Now that is something for you and me to think about today, tomorrow, and for the rest of our lives.

CHAPTER 5

A Business is Born

*When a great person has one object in view to be achieved
in a given time, it may be absolutely necessary for him to
walk out of all the common roads.*
—*Burke*

How could I have ever made it without my dear wife, Dorothy? She was my rock, my friend, confidante, business partner, and dedicated mother to our wonderful children. We were married in 1938, just before we moved to Baltimore to establish my career with Carrier because they saw a greater potential for industrial refrigeration business there than what I had been doing in Bethlehem. When I married Dottie, I knew I had found my soul mate for life.

Everyone who knew her loved Dottie. Our family—especially our ten grandchildren—adored her for the great love she continually showered on them. Our place of refuge in the Poconos, affectionately called The Hottel's Shepherd Cottage, later became our family's refuge: a place to return to after skiing, swimming, water skiing, riding snowmobiles, golf carts, or bicycles, or just passing back and forth to the Lodge. "Me-Mom," a term of endearment used by the grandchildren, always had goodies ready on the table, and everyone felt at home, something they demonstrated on many occasions by freely going to the refrigerator or to the cupboard to help themselves. Dottie was not only big-hearted, sharing everything she had with others, but she also bought things by the dozen or by the cases to be certain she would always have enough on hand for anyone who came by. Her generosity would bring an equally kind response from others, although she never sought anything for herself in return.

Dorothy "Dottie" Hottel

Falling in Love

I was first attracted to Dorothy Gillespie when I observed the business-like responsibility she displayed during her employment as secretary of the school board in Bethlehem. She graduated from high school with high honors and was given a job upon graduation with the school district, where she was dependable and efficient. When I started dating her, however, I soon found I had severe competition: *her working overtime at the office.* She worked at the school board for 15 years before we were married. During that time, Dottie helped her family through the difficult Depression years when Bethlehem Steel virtually closed its doors, leaving most of the city of Bethlehem out of work, including her father, who had no other means by which to support his five school-age children. Dottie's loyalty to her own struggling family during the Depression—never thinking of herself, and waiting to get married until she was past 30—made a deep impression on me. Although I would half-heartedly date other girls, mostly in my dad's church, I always asked myself whom I would rather be with if I had a day off. Whenever I would pick the best girl for good company to go on a holiday trip somewhere, I would always choose Dottie.

Now, these many years later, Dottie would find herself the wife of an employee of Carrier, a man who knew he had found his professional calling in one of the newest, most exciting industries in the country. Even as I write these words, I can feel her tug gently at my heart as I think of that difficult day in February 1982 when Dottie went home to be with her Lord. It is still difficult at times to realize that she is not at my side. During our almost 50 years together, she was my source of strength and support—something I needed as the calls continued to come in like a torrent from clients who saw the need for the unique technology of "handling air like a fluid" that Dr. Willis Carrier had developed.

Still feeling the energy of an entrepreneur running strong in my blood, I knew I could not work for someone else forever. So in 1945, at our dining room table, Dottie and I started Fidelity Engineering Corporation with several former Carrier distributor employees. Dottie had a sterling reputation for being

... We stepped out in faith together to start our new adventure. We had no financial backing and took almost no salary...

diligent and dependable in all her dealings with people. As executive vice president, secretary, and treasurer of our company through many difficult years, she developed an outstanding rapport with customers and large companies from which we purchased millions of dollars of products. At all times, her word was accepted and respected as she would scrutinize the inventory continuously. If there were excess parts and materials from a job site, she made sure they were returned to the shop inventory. Defective items and bad compressors under warranty were returned promptly.

I always said she was one of the world's greatest mothers and the greatest secretary, bookkeeper, and treasurer any little growing company could have as we stepped out in faith together to start our new adventure. We had no financial backing and took almost no salary except what we needed to feed our babies or pay our church dues and mortgage payments. There were times when it was tough to put enough money together to make the employee payroll. But we made it. And I give the lion's share of the credit to Dottie.

> **...the operators and their union organization demanded refrigeration cooling and were threatening an immediate strike...**

After we went out on our own, we continued our engineering schooling, primarily through the Carrier Company, Frigidaire, and a few other manufacturers, so we could stay up with—and get ahead of—the technology of the time. As corporate secretary of Fidelity Engineering Corporation, Dottie was able to do the business full-time and still meet the needs of our daughter, Anne, and our three sons, Jack, Bill and Jim. Dottie was the most productive person I had ever met. She knew how to plan, keep good records, and make sure the important things were always under control. To start a family and a new business at the same time as the war ended took intestinal fortitude and a pure, unadulterated confidence in what we were attempting to do. I know without a doubt that God blessed our efforts and faithfulness because we did our best to keep Him as our first priority.

Averting a Strike

I recall the day I answered an urgent call from a large copper plant in South Baltimore. I was taken upstairs to observe five control rooms where a man operated the controls that throttled the flow of molten hot copper into vertical round containers. When cooled, the containers formed solid three-inch and four-inch thick copper rods that reached to the floor below. The heat was unbearable; it was even worse in those five control rooms. I quickly learned that the operators and their union organization demanded refrigeration cooling and were threatening an immediate strike if their demands were not met. After sweating it out for a few minutes in that environment, I could understand their position. It was an inferno.

After making a heat load calculation, I returned to our shop and discussed this unusual situation with our installation and service technicians. It was critical that we help the company avoid an imminent strike. I called in our top refrigeration installation technician, Melvin Hershberger—the best refrigeration man in Baltimore—who suggested we take five two-ton, air-cooled Frigidaire condensing units from our inventory and change the standard

Freon 22 refrigerant to Freon 12 to reduce the head pressure so it could function efficiently in that extremely hot environment. Melvin's analysis was correct. Not to modify it as he suggested might damage the unit. Once we completed the conversions, we hauled them to the plant and mounted one of the condensing units on the roof of each control room. We also installed an evaporator blower inside on the ceiling with adjustable diffuser veins, along with a temperature control thermostat for the operator to set as he desired. Mission accomplished.

Several months later, we received another urgent call. We were asked to do the same kind of cooling project for a company's 60-foot-high crane operators, who worked over intense flames as they fed trees for firewood from 18-wheelers into a large fire. Molten liquid copper flowed from the fire into plate-type container molds to be removed by the crane for cooling. It really was an inferno for the crane operator.

> **Never had I heard of an air conditioning system installed in a moving crane 60 feet in the air just to please one man...**

Management asked me to have the agreement signed as proof that the crane installation had been let out for contract. They then told me they needed the contract proposal by seven o'clock the following morning—at a union meeting—or the entire plant would go on strike. I already had an eight o'clock appointment at Johns Hopkins Hospital for a brain tumor operation on our son Jack, so I changed my schedule to write up the proposal contract that night for delivery on time *before* the union meeting the following morning.

Here is how we accomplished the task. We made a secure mounting of the compressor on the crane steel frame high up adjacent to the control cabin. We then mounted a horizontal evaporator blower unit high in front of the operator's chair with adjustable diffuser veins so that the control man could blow the cooled air directly on his face and body—which he did to his great satisfaction. We found we were not required to enclose the cab. Never in my life had I heard of an air conditioning system installed in a moving crane 60 feet in the air just to please one man in his control cabin. However, that was our assignment, and we were successful in helping the company avoid a strike, thanks to our skilled installation technicians.

Top-Secret Vessel

On another occasion, while attending our annual ASHRAE Convention in Chicago, I found a note on my bed when I returned to my room to call the sales manager of the Arnot Company, who was in New York. He had recommended me to some ship architects who were designing a new, fast, classified ship for the war effort that was being built at the Newport News shipyards in Norfolk, Virginia. Arnot designed, and would be furnishing, Pullman-type pullout beds for the vessel. It so happened that Arnot's company offices were in the same building as Fidelity Engineering Corporation in Baltimore. I think that is why they knew of our experience in applying refrigeration in unusual war effort applications.

I agreed to leave the convention in Chicago to fly to New York to have dinner with the ship architects around seven o'clock the next evening. Unfortunately, my plane circled New York for more than two hours looking for a hole in the thick fog to land safely. Meanwhile, the folks waiting for me in the hotel were kept informed by radio. Our meeting was delayed for several hours, but the five of us finally met and enjoyed a good dinner and each other's

> **They told me the ship, SS United States, would be a special vessel indeed— its speed a classified secret.**

company. We left the hotel at around eleven and made plans to meet again the following morning at eight.

I arrived at eight o'clock sharp and was led into a beautiful suite that overlooked New York Harbor. They told me the ship, *SS United States,* would be a special vessel indeed—its speed a classified secret. It was so designed that it could be quickly converted into a troop ship with the ability to rush a large number of soldiers wherever they might be needed. We spent the day discussing the various areas on the ship's blueprints that needed to be refrigerated: food storage, kitchen service for the restaurants, and under-the-counter and bar cabinet refrigeration. Most ships at the time used ocean water-cooled compressors located deep in the hull, which circulated a cold water brine through the evaporators in the insulated cabinets and walk-in coolers.

We all agreed it would be most desirable if we could eliminate the insulated piping to and from the chiller in the hull to all the small cabinet evaporators. However, it would be necessary to locate a small space for the different areas to mount the air-cooled remote condensing units so the hot condenser discharge air would escape. When we took our seats around the large table, we each found before us a detailed typed copy of our discussion from the night before, when we had first spoken of the design of an air-cooled type system. I imagine a copy of our deliberations also was sent to the Newport News shipyards.

The next day I returned to the office to prepare a complete folder of all the items to be included in our proposal, with detailed specifications: dimensions, current characteristics and installation instructions, and extra spare parts, including pictures of the equipment to be sent both to the New

SS United States – highly classified special ship; food storage and kitchen refrigeration designed by Clarence W. Hottel

York architects and to the shipyards. Included were our factory-printed prices for their approval. We discovered the shipyard people were quite fussy about what they approved: they asked us to include a spare part for *every item they might need to replace for service.* They requested that these items be sealed and mailed in waterproof heavy wax paper. They also asked for a complete folder on instructions for the installation and maintenance of all equipment used on this classified ship on its top-secret missions.

The Foundation for Good Business

Harvey and I had learned in our teen years that customers believed in us *in proportion to the way we knew our business; provided good, honest, prompt service; and put their installations into operation at peak efficiency.* After Dottie and I started Fidelity Engineering Corporation, I continued to think a great deal about the work ethic we had both developed early in our lives. Again, I was grateful to parents who modeled that kind of honest consistency—a foundation and philosophy for living that never let Harvey or me down. I also knew that success would depend on my ability to infuse and instill in my people a respect for, and a strong belief in, the power of creativity. That, too, I trust is seen as one of the strengths of Fidelity Engineering Corporation even today.

One afternoon I received a call from a Coast Guard engineer who asked me to help him design a special room they were adding on one of their ships. When I arrived on location, I found him trying to apply a window unit, which would have been impossible. After I had an opportunity to show why such a configuration would not work—and demonstrated the type of equipment that would—a full-dressed Navy captain came by, stood over us, and gave me his approval to proceed with what I had suggested. This was top priority for the Coast Guard. The room had been designed with a large, uninsulated metal dome that measured approximately 18 feet. My suspicion was that it might be coded signal equipment. I knew Coast Guard ships could go close to their targets to access information and then signal coded data to headquarters before making a landing. Somewhat to my surprise, Carrier, York, and Trane refused to make a special unit for us from their assembly line to give us all-copper coils for the condenser and evaporator, instead of the more commonly used aluminum. I was confident that copper would have greater endurance as the ship's deck would on occasion be sprayed with salt water and exposed to brackish air.

> **My suspicion was that it might be coded signal equipment.**

Fortunately, we were able to persuade Lennox to build special copper coil units for this unique assignment—a seven-and-a-half-ton system. When the equipment arrived, together with my sons Bill and Jim and a couple of our best mechanics, we mounted the air-cooled equipment, ran the copper piping to the blower units in the sealed, secret room, and fitted the electric wiring to the controls. It performed to spec, as we were sure it would. This adaptation eliminated the need for a special salt water-cooling compressor down in the hull, and the normal insulated piping brine circulating water to the evaporator blowers in the sealed room. The Coast Guard was so pleased with the work of our team that they sent one ship after another in for the same installation. In all, five Coast Guard ships were ultimately equipped with our air-cooled condensing unit design, rather than the traditional salt water-cooling compressor.

Years earlier I remember seeing a large sign high above the podium in front of a classroom in the Syracuse plant, where Dr. Willis Carrier himself taught us the science of thermodynamics as it was being applied to mechanical refrigeration. The sign read: CARRIER KNOWS THE ART OF HANDLING AIR. This sign made an indelible impression on me, and I never forgot its message. I was confident at that time that I, too, would one day master the art of handling air like a fluid. As I grew into my profession, I knew I would have multiple opportunities to demonstrate innovative techniques in handling air. One such time was at Aberdeen Proving Ground, where we installed refrigeration in a test room that had enough capacity to maintain

> I remember going into that room at −70° F when it was first started up just to see how it felt. I came out quickly!

0º F, at which temperature they would fire at a tank in simulated frigid weather operational conditions; they also needed to simulate an environment that rose to 140º F. In addition, they would fire at a thick armored plate at high and low temperatures, testing the damage on both the steel armor plate and the projectile. Our analysis and application worked. Later, we designed and installed a room refrigerated to maintain –70º F. This room was used to test the powder of a newly designed bazooka that would also be test fired under both extremely hot and frigid temperatures. I remember going into that room at –70º F when it was first started up just to see how it felt. I came out quickly!

We later learned the Germans had been completely stalled in their attempt to invade and capture Moscow *because of their inability to engage in combat at such extremely low temperatures.* Hitler's storm troopers and their tons of armory had literally frozen in their tracks, unable to advance. Because of what we were able to accomplish, it was my hope that our soldiers would never be placed in such jeopardy. All this was simply another contribution our Carrier team was able to make to the war effort—something we did gladly as patriots in a war we knew we must win!

How Air Conditioning Works

There are times when the buyer asks questions about the theory of refrigeration, and you are obliged to explain that the major components of an air conditioning system are a compressor, a condenser, an evaporator, and Freon (or equivalent) fluid refrigerant held under pressure (see diagram following page or color diagram on page xviii, courtesy of the Henry Valve Company). The Freon evaporates when the pressure is released by a thermostatic expansion valve into the low-pressure coils of the evaporator. It becomes a gas, and its temperature drops sharply. The Freon, now a cold gas, absorbs heat from the indoor room through the evaporator coils. As it moves through the coils to the compressor, the Freon liquefies and the liquid gives up its heat to the outside air through the condenser coils.

The Freon is now cooled and is returned to the compressor, where this process is repeated continually, moving heat from the inside air to the outdoors whenever the compressor is running. This blast of hot air released by the outside condenser indicates the great amount of heat exchange.

The British Thermal Unit (BTU) is the amount of heat necessary to raise the temperature of one pound of pure water one degree Fahrenheit. When you hear that a condensing unit is so many tons, it has nothing to do with the weight of the machinery and equipment; 12,000 BTUs is a ton of refrigeration, and if an application is designed to guarantee 75º F inside when it is 95º F outside, the total heat load in BTUs will determine the size of the compressor and matching equipment.

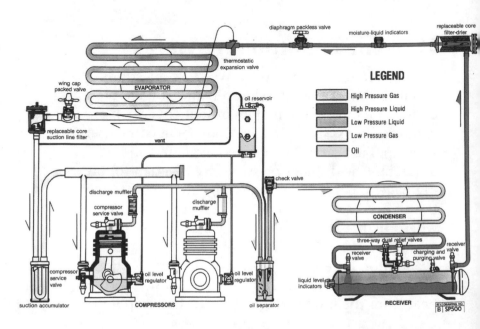

It has been the successful application of these principles of air conditioning—and a commitment to excellence in customer service—that has made Fidelity Engineering Corporation the company it is today, and that is positioning it for even greater success in the years ahead.

A Commitment to Excellence

As our young company took emerging technology to new levels, I became increasingly aware that unless we remained *on the edge* of all technical development, were ever vigilant on maintaining our *learning curve,* and demanded constant excellence from ourselves and our products, we simply could not thrive in what was now becoming a burgeoning industry. Egos would need to be put aside and we would have to trash outmoded obstructions to the creative process. While we had our all-important, trusty operational manuals, we also knew we had to think beyond the current problems to what might be even more effective solutions. We also knew part of our challenge was to encourage our clients to begin "thinking outside the box." Sometimes we were successful, sometimes not. Most important, we needed to remain humble in the face of our many challenges and not take our many successes for granted.

> **Egos would need to be put aside and we would have to trash outmoded obstructions to the creative process.**

Years later, I would read Oswald Chambers, who wrote in *Disciples Needed* these stirring words:

Nothing in connection with our personality is so disastrously enervating as disillusionment about ourselves. We much prefer our own idea of ourselves to the stern realization of what we really are. [The apostle] Paul warns, "Let no man think of himself more highly than he ought to think." Watch how God has disillusioned you over yourself and see the value of it for the future . . . individuality can never become a sacrament, it is only personality that can become a sacrament through oneness with Jesus Christ.

It's Not the Critic Who Counts

As a child, Teddy Roosevelt was thin and asthmatic. His father said, "Theodore, you have the mind but not the body, and without the body the mind cannot go as far as it should. *You must make your body.* It is hard drudgery to make one's body, but I know you will do it." Teddy followed his father's words and developed his body. Years later he wrote:

It is not the critic who counts, not the man who points out how the strong man stumbled, or where the doer of deeds could have done them better. The credit belongs to the man who is actually in the arena; whose face is marred by dust and sweat and blood; who strives valiantly, who errs and comes short again and again; who knows the great enthusiasms, the great devotions, and spends himself in a worthy cause; who, at the best, knows in the end the triumph of high achievement; and who at the worst, at least fails while daring greatly, so that his place shall never be with those cold and timid souls who know neither victory nor defeat.

I hope that you, my reader friend, will never be one of these cold and timid souls who know neither victory nor defeat. Rather, it is my prayer that you will devote your days to doing your best work, surrounding your efforts with great enthusiasm, so that in the end your high achievement may be great indeed.

CHAPTER 6

Working through the Pain

Men who fear God face life fearlessly.
Men who do not fear God end up fearing everything.
—*Richard Halverson*

I n the summer of 1954 ,when Jack, our oldest son, was 12 years old, we received a call from Sandy Cove Conference Center to come to the Boys Camp area. The person in charge said, "Mr. Hottel, Jack has fallen from his horse and we have him in sick bay." I quickly left my office in Baltimore and went to the camp in North East, Maryland. I learned that my three sons—Jack, Bill, and Jim—had been riding together with Jack in the lead. Bill and Jim told

Jack, Bill, Jim and Anne swimming at Ocean City, Maryland – 1953

me how Jack's harness had broken loose, and how, with his harness still in hand, he had fallen backwards, striking the back of his head on the road. We took Jack home and had him checked immediately by our family physician, Dr. Carl Myers, who examined his head bruise and body reactions. He recommended medication and rest.

Before long, however, we noticed that Jack was having difficulty standing erect and keeping his balance. When he finally returned to class, his friends would have to carry his books as he struggled through his high school classes, always a bit off balance and always fearful of falling. It was difficult for the entire family, but tougher for Jack, who pushed through those trying years so valiantly, forced to depend on his family and friends to help him. Finally, he had to resort to a wheelchair to get around.

Jack Hottel at age 14

For years after, we continued to make one arrangement after another for specialists to examine and test our son. We were fortunate to be living in Baltimore, the home of Johns Hopkins Hospital, where many of these tests were administered. I recall the many meetings we had to determine what should be done to relieve the apparent buildup of a pressure-like tumor in a section of our son's brain. Ultimately, Jack, his doctors—who had now studied Jack's problem for months—and Dottie and me decided that it would be best to operate and remove the pressure and restriction that caused his lack of balance and control.

The Surgery

Dottie and I stayed at the Sheraton Hotel across the street from the hospital before and after the operation so we could be with Jack as much as we were allowed. After the brain surgery, the doctors gave us permission to be with him for only five minutes at a time. When the drugs finally wore off, I thought I saw a good sign of potential recovery, and with my usual positive approach to life, I said to the doctor, "Say, don't you think Jack looks better already?" I will never forget the doctor's answer. He turned to me and said, "If Jack is any better it would have to come from above." That remark told me that positive thinking alone would not bring our son back. Obviously, the doctor was not pleased with the result of his work. I was immediately fearful that the surgery may have disturbed the inner ear nerve to Jack's brain.

After several more weeks in the hospital, we brought Jack home and made further arrangements to take him to other hospitals where highly recommended specialists would observe and test him. Gradually, however, Jack lost his sight. Over time we helped him learn to use a Braille typewriter on which he wrote letters to those people he loved. Sadly, Jack finally lost his hearing, although he could continue to speak rather well.

A Fellowship of Friends

Dr. John Evans, the leader of our weekly Baltimore Breakfast Group, carried one of Jack's letters with him at all times, often telling our fellowship that it was the most precious piece of correspondence he had ever received. My friend Abraham Vereide, an immigrant pioneer of Christian leadership and the founder of the prayer breakfast movement in our nation, would always urge me to bring Jack to our small-group teaching meetings. Next to my own father, I consider Dr. Abraham Vereide a man who most impressed me with his kind, humble leadership, which helped me change the direction of my life. If you have not read his book *Modern Viking,* I urge you to read it as soon as possible.

> **Bill and Jim had to lift Jack in and out of his wheelchair as he grew weaker and unable to go it alone.**

Dr. Vereide was sensitive to the Spirit of God wherever He might manifest Himself, and he knew God's seal of blessing was on the Breakfast Groups wherever they would meet. He also knew there would always be new sacrifices for us to make as believers. He was realistic enough to recognize that additional strains and stresses on our normal routine of life would be present at all times. Dr. Vereide remained sensitive to the needs of individuals to the end of his life. I am sure that is why God used him so mightily for so long, not only with us who were just "common" persons, but also with our nation's presidents, members of Congress, and with so many others who shared the national spotlight. He would often remind us of the verse from the Bible that says, "'Except a grain of wheat fall into the ground and *die,* it abideth alone; but if it die, it bringeth forth much fruit'" (John 12:24, KJV, emphasis mine). I often wondered if that verse might one day be prophetic for my son, Jack.

Whenever we traveled as a family to places such as Sandy Cove or Pinebrook Camp or to our summer home in the Poconos, Bill and Jim had to lift Jack in and out of his wheelchair as he grew weaker and unable to go it alone. During this difficult time, Jack would often recite his favorite Bible verse, Romans 10:13: "For whosoever shall call upon the name of the Lord shall be saved." He had memorized this special portion of Scripture years before when he was still able to hear and see. Quoting that verse with a heart full of Christian love and boundless cheer, he would tell others that he would one day be with his Lord forever.

A Future Family Reunion

Nellie, our faithful full-time housekeeper, and I decided it was time to call the doctor who had performed the surgery. We believed Jack was on the way to leaving us to be with his Lord. His mother knew it; she was crying and went upstairs to her bedroom. Nellie was one of Jack's best friends. She said she would clean him up so Jack would be ready for the doctor to examine him.

...there was a deep sense of joy to realize Jack's soul was with the Lord.

On Sunday morning, September 20, 1964, our precious son went to be with his Lord and Savior. He was 23 years old. Jack had been a strong, firm, no-nonsense type of boy with top leadership qualities. It was my plan to encourage him to continue his education and become our company CPA, heading up the office as his mother had done. But such was not to be.

I learned that Johns Hopkins specialty surgeons do not like to sign a death certificate, but this doctor had made many recent visits to check on Jack at our home and knew more about our son than anyone else. He finally agreed to come and sign the certificate stating that Jack had died.

The entire Hottel family was there, and of course we were very sad. But there was a deep sense of joy to realize Jack's soul was with the Lord. He often assured us that he was a born-again believer of the scriptures he had memorized.

Our Pastor, Rev. Robert C. Bradford of Maryland Presbyterian Church, was much loved by our family, particularly Dorothy. He brought comfort and assurance of God's love and care. We were all active church members, so the prayers and love of our church family, as well as the Baltimore Breakfast Group, were appreciated and very comforting.

Rev. Robert C. Bradford and Clarence Hottel in 1967

Dorothy's family, the Gillespies, was always very much concerned about Jack. He was born in Bethlehem, Pennsylvania, where they still lived. We made many trips together there to visit. The Gillespie grandparents treated him as though he was their son, and now that he had died, you can imagine how sad they were and how hard they took the news. We all had to learn that God permitted this to happen and that Jack's soul is with Him and with our many loved ones, for all eternity, time without end. Thank the Lord!

Today, as I write these words, I look forward to that day when I will be reunited with Jack, Dottie, my dad and mother, my brother Winfred, and my twin brother, Harvey, along with the hundreds of Christian friends who have gone before. It is also my constant prayer that our family circle will be unbroken, and that all will find their way into the ark of safety before Christ returns, or before any one of us is called from this world of unbelief to be forever with Him. For at that time, Satan and his sting of death will be conquered and we will praise Jesus' name forever.

As I look through my bookshelf, I am heartened even now as I read the fitting words of Charles Swindoll from his book *David*. Swindoll writes,

> *Some of you who read these pages are in the process of having every crutch removed from your life. This creates enormous pain and instability when support we had counted on is torn from us. For some, it is represented by a broken romance. The man or woman you felt was God's choice has now vanished, and it hurts deeply. . . . For some, it has been the death of a dream. Everything you hoped and planned for has gone up in smoke. Now, you have a choice. You can look around for some other something or someone to lean on—or you can lean on God, and God ALONE.* Charles Swindoll, *David*. Word Publishing (Dallas: 1997), p. 69.

The Business Continues

Losing a loved one is devastating. However, life must go on for the living. One day, the McCormick Company (a spice corporation) called and asked us to meet with them as soon as possible at a proposed job site where a large walk-in cooler was to be built from the ground up. Our challenge was to design and insulate a facility that could maintain

35º F temperature year-round. The interior of the cooler would be 50' x 50' x 14', with no poles or beams. We immediately contacted a factory in Scranton, Pennsylvania, which specialized in prefab insulated panels for cool rooms and freezers. The design drawings were approved, and within five weeks the entire assembly, including the necessary steel beams for the high ceiling, was ready for installation. I can still see those two 18-wheelers drive up with the beams, 16-foot insulated wall panels, large sliding door, and floor and ceiling panels—all of which fit beautifully in place just as we had marked on our drawings.

> **I do not think we used the word *self-esteem* much in those days...**

Within six days, when all the equipment arrived, we completed the refrigeration compressors and air handlers, and the storage room was ready. We were all delighted at what we were able to accomplish in such a short time for such a large room, and happy that McCormick, a good, regular customer, was pleased.

I do not think we used the word *self-esteem* much in those days, although it is a concept much in vogue today. However, if we had, I would have told you self-esteem and the capacity to feel good about oneself is not magic. If anything, it is a product. The steps to building a good self-esteem are not much different from building an air conditioning or heating unit. First, one must understand the basic "anatomy" of what one is trying to build. Once that is grasped, the most important part of the project has been completed. The analogy is this. God created our bodies, our spirits, and our souls with love and a capacity for hard work and goodness. The hard work, if you like, has already been done for us. Now, *who we think we are is an indicator of what we feel we are worth.* It is my avowed belief that we have value *because of what God has done for us,* which means we really have no option other than to see ourselves as a product of *positives.* That is how we felt about ourselves in the early days of our business. Yes, we had setbacks. No, we did not get all the contracts we bid on. However, none of this slowed us down because we knew we had given our lives and our future to God. Our "self-esteem" was in tact in Him.

Sleeping in the Bank

One hot June morning I received a call from Victor Frenkil, president of Baltimore Contractors, Inc., asking me to pick him up at ten o'clock at his office on South Central Avenue. I parked at his front door and he jumped in the car.

"Where are we going?" I asked.

"We have an appointment at First National Bank."

I kept driving. When we arrived at the bank, he said, "Just drive into the side alley and lock the car."

"But I'll be blocking the alley," I protested.

Victor responded, "No problem. It's the bank's alley."

All Vic Frenkil had said up to now was that he wanted me to meet these fellows. After entering the revolving door, we noticed the first front office to our right belonged to the chairman of the board, Walter Graham. He was just emerging from a meeting, and with him were the president and vice president, all seemingly eager to meet with us. After a few moments of greeting and hand shaking, Frenkil said, "Whatever Mr. Hottel recommends you do for your bank's air conditioning needs, I will guarantee it 100 percent." Who would not enjoy a vote of confidence such as that!

After some general conversation, the subject of ductwork came up, which, the bank officers assumed, would spoil the artful appearance of their beautifully decorated 100-foot-long high ceiling. As I sized up the situation, I told them my plan would be to mount the air handling blower units high above the rear mezzanine with special adjustable discharge diffusers that would reach the full 100 feet to the front entrance. I told them the 45-foot-high ceiling would make this type of design possible. I also promised them there would be no noise or drafts since the 60º F conditioned air discharge would be blown high; by the time it dropped into all the open ceiling offices and open tellers' side of the bank, the temperatures would average 75º F when it was 95º out-

"They are politicians; we are bankers," he shot back.

side. I promised we would guarantee all Carrier-recommended comfort zone chart conditions.

Chairman Graham called me into his office and asked several questions about my family, my company, and me. Over the course of the next few minutes we became quite friendly. In fact, he kept me there with him while he was still tending to others who were standing in front of us. When he finally broke free of his other obligations, he asked me where I banked.

I said, "Across the street at Maryland National."

"They are politicians; we are bankers," he shot back.

He then took me to one of his young tellers and said to her, "Miss, put $10,000 in Mr. Hottel's Fidelity Engineering Corporation account." He then gave me a receipt in a bankbook. After this quick and surprising financial transaction, we returned to his office.

"Because I am armed with the right information, I always come out of the meeting with what I want."

Mr. Graham told me he made sure he always had all the information he needed before he would go into a bank board meeting with any request. Then he said, "Because I am armed with the right information, I always come out of the meeting with what I want." I had a suspicion that he wanted the records to show that Fidelity Engineering Corporation had an account with First National Bank.

It did not take me long to prepare a cost sheet and a proposal contract for our intended project. After making a total heat load calculation and deciding on the type of equipment that would be necessary, I determined we could avoid the tremendous cost of rigging and mounting the evaporative condenser on the roof. Otherwise, we would be cutting through 20 floors for the interconnecting piping that would lead to the condensing compressor unit in the basement. I also engineered the job so the liquid and hot gas lines from the condensing unit to the air handlers in the mezzanine would be eliminated. Instead, we would apply a new, recently developed high tonnage air-cooled package unit completely assembled at the factory, ready to plug in and run when connected to proper three-phase electric power.

I arranged with Vic's carpenters to enclose the room completely with enough space for service and a change of filters. Upon completion of the project, customers would enter the bank and neither see nor hear the air conditioning. They would only feel the pleasant cooling that made banking a pleasure. I promised Mr. Graham we would

> *Vic told me, "You do the right thing for Mr. Graham, and your company will have it made in Baltimore."*

have the entire system up and running by the time he returned from his Fourth of July vacation. This was such a major undertaking that I decided to sleep in the bank the night before to make certain everything was completed and working 100 percent when he returned. I was also protecting my newly deposited $10,000!

Vic told me, "You do the right thing for Mr. Graham, and your company will have it made in Baltimore."

Because of the success of the project, most of the occupants in the building also called Fidelity Engineering Corporation for their air conditioning needs. Of course, Mr. Graham recommended our company to all the tenants because he and his bank people had been so pleased with the work of our engineering team. My dad and mother were visiting us at the time, and it was one of the great thrills of my life to drive down Charles Street, pass the leading bank on the busiest corner of the city, and show them the Fidelity Engineering signs on the front and side walls that read ANOTHER FIDELITY AIR CONDITIONING CORPORATION INSTALLATION FOR FIRST NATIONAL BANK. Those were the days when we always placed our signs on the buildings we were air conditioning. However, more and better jobs were yet to come.

Cooling Bombay

Those of us old enough can recall in the late 1930s and early 1940s the unsightly, noisy water-spraying, redwood cooling towers placed on roofs and in the backyards of virtually every air conditioning installation larger than three-ton capacity. Several manufacturers, the leader of which was the US AIRCO Manufacturing Company, developed a line of package units that included the compressor and evaporative condenser completely interconnected and securely mounted with all parts and electric controls in a package ready to plug in upon delivery at the job site. Their line eventually was available from three to 50 tons, and all models included an air-cooled type condenser, which included a wet spray over the fins of the condenser coils to increase its efficiency. We sold and installed so many of these units that the president of US AIRCO, Mr. Feinberg, gave us an exclusive agreement and an extra percentage discount. We had the advantage over competition particularly in the high-rise office and insurance and bank buildings, where the tenants had to buy their own air conditioning system.

127

Mr. Feinberg called me several times to meet him in New York, the day after his company's annual board meeting. We would have lunch together at the hotel where he stayed to discuss our many applications: where these units were installed, and what we could suggest for improving their design. He told me several times, "If we had 50 dealers like Fidelity in the United States, US AIRCO would be the largest air conditioning manufacturer in the country." US AIRCO was now receiving orders for these package units as far away as Bombay, India— the Blue Ball Plumbing Company. The owner's son, a college graduate, came to work with Fidelity installation and service technicians for about a year to learn how we apply and maintain installations so he could learn how the operation could be carried out in his country.

Places like The May Company, First National Bank of Maryland, The McCormick Company, WJZ-TV, and many restaurants, stores, bowling alleys, and high office building tenants were glad to learn there was a new method of air conditioning without the costly

Bill and Jim during the late 1960s with a Baltimore Rigging high crane lifting a 50-ton unit into the fifth floor of the McCormick Building. This new method of airconditioning eliminated costly piping and unattractive spray towers.

128

piping and unattractive spray towers. (See the picture on page 14.)

Skating on Hard Ice

For several years in the 1930s a popular show played nightly in the New Yorker Hotel ballroom featuring the "Guy Lombardo and his Royal Canadians" orchestra and a famous ice dancer. When the skater had completed her routine, the staff would quickly cover the ice rink by unrolling a slatted wood flooring that went over the ice so the dinner guests could dance until the next show on ice was scheduled.

> ...the Belvedere mechanical engineer...was confident we could work out a plan to provide the indoor ice rink, just as in New York.

The Belvedere Hotel invited the popular show to Baltimore. Thus, it would require the same kind of ice rink. I remember the day we received a call from the Belvedere mechanical engineer who knew me, trusted me, and was confident we could work out a plan to provide the indoor ice rink, just as had been done in New York.

Here's what we did. We cut the floor the size they specified and installed a large, two-and-a-half-inch-deep waterproof pan in which we placed Kold Hold Freon flat evaporator plates, interconnected with adjustable thermal expansion valves on each plate. Then we ran copper refrigerant Freon lines to the floor below, where two five-horsepower Carrier water-cooled compressors were located. We then filled the pan with water to cover the plates, forming a two-inch-thick perfect ice rink. This show ran nightly for two weeks—with a crowded dining room every night!

Sweetheart of a Deal

Mr. Joseph Schapiro was president of a large machine shop in South Baltimore that also manufactured a patented unit for producing edible cones that held ice cream. Mr. Schapiro gave me a call one morning saying he wanted to talk with me right away. When I arrived at his office, both the company's chief engineer and Mr. Schapiro showed me a newly planned conveyer designed to move a fast-moving line of paper cups hanging upside down on hooks as they were drawn past a spray of 500º-hot paraffin. The paraffin would coat the cups inside out as they cooled, after which they moved along a conveyer 90 feet to dry. They would then be ready to be nested together. And therein lay the challenge: the company needed refrigeration cold enough so the cups would not stick together as they were boxed in large cartons and on to waiting trucks for delivery throughout the United States. The demand for delivery was far greater than production. Here is where the Sweetheart cup was born with our application of Carrier low-temperature refrigeration.

...the Sweetheart cup was born with our application of Carrier low-temperature refrigeration.

Our design recommendation to speed up the run would require low-temperature refrigeration immediately after the blast of hot wax. We did this by mounting a Carrier low-temp blast blower unit diffusing 34º F cooling air on the 500º-hot cups as the moving conveyer made its complete turn, going back the 90-foot run in the cold-insulated return tunnel duct, where the shipper found the Sweetheart cups dry and non-sticky, nested and boxed for immediate shipment. They were so pleased with our efforts that they gave me a purchase order for another system. To increase the speed to turn out even more cups per hour, it was necessary to raise the hot wax temperature and use a larger Carrier condensing unit and blower.

> "You sit down and write all the items we need for the larger system and I will sign it."

During the operation, the president came into the room and heard the chief engineer object to the increase in size on the next unit, saying it was not necessary. That's when the president asked me to step into the adjoining room, where he gave me a blank company purchase order and said, "You sit down and write all the items we need for the larger system and I will sign it." Since this happened many years ago, I am not certain, but I believe they ordered yet a third unit with a third increase in size to try to keep up with the demands for their orders before they moved to their new location in Reisterstown, Maryland.

It was amazing to see the large rolls of paper start in the line, and then be cut and printed for such products as popcorn or soft drinks. Next they went from the drying room to the machine room that made the cups ready for the hot wax spray, and then on to the 90-foot cooling tunnel to be nested and prepared for shipment. While watching the complete system in operation, the president asked me to stop at his home at eight o'clock the following morning, which I did.

When I rang the bell of his mansion the next day, he opened the door and welcomed me. Still dressed in his nightwear, he turned around and walked to the kitchen. I followed him, wondering what in the world we were going to talk about.

He then surprised me by asking, "How do you like your eggs?"

"Either scrambled or sunny-side up—with toast," I said.

He then made breakfast for both of us. After we had eaten, he said he wanted to take me to his son's home—a prominent Baltimore doctor—to work on an air conditioning system that needed new equipment or repairs. How could I say no!

Working with the Best

Looking back at the many important decisions I made as owner of a growing business, I have learned to appreciate the wisdom of my friend and experienced attorney—and qualified CPA—Julian Johnson, who has since moved to Virginia. I now enjoy, in much the same manner, the professional services of my esteemed colleague Henry Roesser of the firm Jameson & Associates. We also attribute much of the growth and success of Fidelity Engineering Corporation to the sound advice and personal interest of Morris A. Baker, a terrific friend and wise attorney who guided our little company from its start (which put us on a sound, firm foundation) until he retired.

Only after his retirement did we turn to Robert J. Thieblot and the firm Thieblot, Ryan, Martin & Miller, located in The World Trade Center in Baltimore. Bob always made me feel welcome whenever I went to see him, and Fidelity Engineering Corporation's sound growth, making it one of the largest of its kind in the eastern United States, is evidence of Bob Thieblot's wise counsel in the many important decisions made over the years. Now that Bob has retired, we are privileged to enjoy the services of his close associate, Thomas J. Schetelich. Tom continues to provide the same close friendship and counsel

Referrals and relationships are what successful repeat business is all about.

through his firm, Ferguson, Schetelich & Heffernan, located in the NationsBank Center in downtown Baltimore. Tom is also heading up a qualified Christian committee that will gradually permit my retirement from the responsibility of sponsoring the annual Mayor's/Governor's Prayer Breakfast (usually held at the Baltimore Convention Center), as well as the monthly breakfast meetings held by the Baltimore Fellowship Foundation, known as the Baltimore Breakfast Group. These meetings have been held regularly since the days of President Eisenhower (1952).

Friendship and Business

Referrals and relationships are what successful repeat business is all about. I was invited to that president's house for a non-business breakfast, and because we had done solid work for him and his company, he gave us even more business. It is an axiom that *people want to do business with people they respect and trust.* Think for a moment of those with whom you want to do business, and I am sure you will agree. That is why integrity is the key to the success of any venture— large or small. Then, following on this spirit of trustworthiness comes one of the greatest prizes of all: friendships that often last

PEOPLE WANT TO DO BUSINESS WITH PEOPLE THEY RESPECT AND TRUST.

a lifetime. Friendship carries with it the joys of mutual understanding that help to make life colorful, interesting, and rewarding. You can never replace a friend. When people are fortunate enough to have several, they discover they are all different. *No one has a double in friendship!* This philosophy has been a success formula for Fidelity Engineering Corporation from day one; it is still the way we continue to do business today. To underline what I mean, I want to leave you with these special thoughts:

A little more kindness and a little less creed;

A little more giving and a little less greed;

A little more smile and a little less frown;

A little less kicking of the one who is down;

A little more "we" and a little less "I";

A little more flowers on the pathway of life;

And fewer on graves at the end of the strife.

After living a life rich with friends and business associates for more than 90 years, I can say without fear of contradiction that this is a sure blueprint for personal and business success. May it also be the substance of your life and work today and throughout the even better years still to come for you, the reader, and the valued employees of Fidelity Engineering Corporation.

"Beautiful babies".
Harvey and Clarence
born August 6, 1908,
Fleetwood, PA.

Franklin Hottel Family, 1916,
Philadelphia, PA.

Family Outing. "See Dad's
proud boys in Overland!"
1920, Philadelphia, PA.

FAMILY

The Franklin Hottel Family lived in Philadelphia (Grayce and Winfred, the second set of twins, are 2 years old), 1922.

Franklin Hottel Family, 1926: Back row, l to r- Harvey, Verletta, Clarence. Center- Ruth. Front row, l to r- Mother, Grayce, Winfred, and Dad, Bethlehem, PA.

Family Time with the Clarence Hottel Family, 1947. Clarence and Dorothy with Bill, Jack, Jim and Anne.

A Family Christmas Greeting, 1956 (l to r) Anne, Bill, Jim, Dorothy, Jack and Clarence, Baltimore, MD.

FAMILY

Anne and Jack in Children's Choir.

The three boys (Jack, Bill and Jim) with Grandpa, 1958.

Ralph and Grayce Reed (Grayce is Clarence's younger sister),1954.

Hottel children with Grandpa in a boat, 1951.

Bill and Sally's wedding, 1965, Baltimore, MD.

Jim and Kathy, 1966, Baltimore, MD.

Anne and John Turnbull's wedding, 1969.

FAMILY

Mother and Dad's 50th wedding anniversary, 1956. Front row: Harvey, Mom, Dad, and Clarence. Back row: Ruth, Winfred, Verletta, and Grayce.

Dad's 75th Birthday, 1957.

Henry and Jennifer Cabell after church (Clarence's two oldest grandchildren. Anne is their mother), 1968.

Clarence and his Mother on Mother's day 1968.

Mother on her 88th birthday, August 3, 1976.

Clarence and his Mother, 1977.

FAMILY

Our two sets of twins at Harvey's Piper Twin Engine plane, 1969.

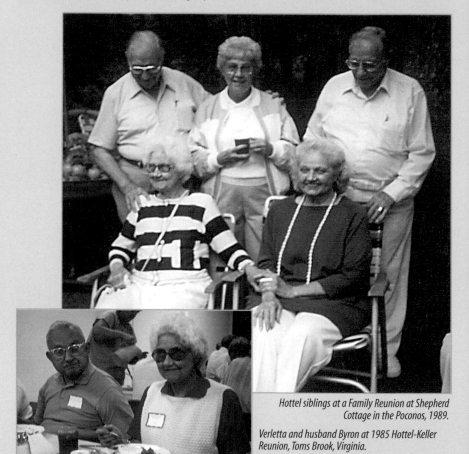

Hottel siblings at a Family Reunion at Shepherd Cottage in the Poconos, 1989.

Verletta and husband Byron at 1985 Hottel-Keller Reunion, Toms Brook, Virginia.

Harvey and Clarence at the Congressional Country Club, Bethesda, MD, early 1950s.

Vacationing at St. Maarten, 1986.

Harvey and Clarence's 80th Birthday celebration at the home of Dick and Marge Hottel, 1988.

FAMILY

Harvey and Clarence receive birthday gifts— everything in twos, 1985.

Harvey and Clarence on a retirement cruise to Alaska, 1990.

90th Birthday celebration, 1998.

Harvey and Clarence with Bob Larson (interview for the book), 1999.

Jim and Kathy Hottel at the Fidelity
40th Anniversay Banquet, 1985.

Holiday Open House at my home with grandchildren Chris, Carrie,
and Mike (Jim Hottel's children), 1991.

First great grandson, Devan Christopher Ortiz, 1999.

Granddaughter Christine with my second great
grandson, Nathaniel Alexander Ortiz, 1999.

Holding my great grand-
daughter, Tiara Marie Ortiz
(one day old), 1999.

FAMILY

Anne and John Turnbull, 1996.

Granddaughter Kate's wedding (John Turnbull Family), October 2000.

Winfred's Family (Winfred went to be with the Lord in 1972).

Dorothy Hottel (left) with her sisters, Anamae, Betty, and Marietta.

Marietta's (Dorothy Hottel's sister) and Hazel's (sister-in-law) 80th Birthday Family Reunion, 1990.

FAMILY

Bill Hottel's family,
late 1980s.

Nancy Hottel's graduation at
Gettysburg College, 1992.

Clarence and Harvey at Beth and Mike Palumbo's wedding, 1993.

Clarence with granddaughter
Beth and great granddaughter
Emily Anne Palumbo, 1997.

Bill with his first
grandchild, Emily.

Holding my fifth great grandchild, Madeleine Claire Palumbo (10 days old), July 2000.

THE HOTTEL BROTHERS

Hottel Brothers store, 520 West Broad Street, Bethlehem,PA, Late 1920s.

Hottel Brothers new truck, in the 1920s.

Both Hottel Brothers became chairmen of the Washington-Baltimore ASRE. Group photo of past chairmen (l to r) Clarence W. Hottel 1949-50, T. Shotton, Jr. 1947-48, William S. Woodside 1944-45, Arthur C. Crawford 1948-49, Ruben E. Ottenheimer 1940-41, Walter H. Volker 1945-46, William J. Dugas 1946-47, Harvey W. Hottel 1943-44.

Portraits of Clarence and Dorothy Hottel, who founded Fidelity Engineering Corporation on their dining room table in 1945.

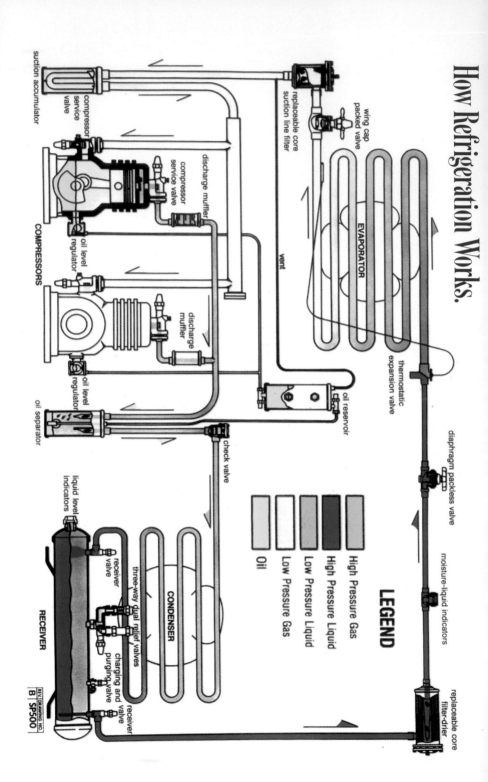

How Refrigeration Works.

COMPRESSORS

suction accumulator

compressor service valve

oil level regulator

discharge muffler

compressor service valve

discharge muffler

oil level regulator

oil separator

check valve

replaceable core suction line filter

wing cap packed valve

EVAPORATOR

thermostatic expansion valve

vent

oil reservoir

diaphragm packless valve

moisture-liquid indicators

replaceable core filter-drier

liquid level indicators

receiver valve

three-way dual relief valves

CONDENSER

charging and purging valve

receiver valve

RECEIVER

LEGEND

High Pressure Gas

High Pressure Liquid

Low Pressure Liquid

Low Pressure Gas

Oil

REV. DRAWING NO.

B | **SP500**

The Refrigeration Service Engineer

VOL. 12   NO. 1   ★ ★ ★   JANUARY . 1944

PIPE AND TUBE BENDING •

NEWS OF WAR REGULATIONS •

POST-WAR REFRIGERATORS •

Clarence Hottel is pictured on the cover checking the pressure and temperature gauge readings to maintain constant 100 degree below zero refrigeration installation at the John Hopkins Laboratory, 1944.

FIDELITY ENGINEERING

Fidelity's 40th Anniversary Banquet at Marriott's Hunt Valley Inn Ballroom, (l to r) Bill, Clarence and Jim Hottel, 1985.

Three generations of Hottels: Clarence, Bill and Beth, 1995.

Entrance to 25 Loveton Circle.

150 big and small trucks on the road ready to serve.

McCormick Company 1000 KW generator installation (Hunt Valley location). Kohler Technicians Karl Giannicinni and David Dougherty with Clarence Hottel, 1980s.

FIDELITY ENGINEERING

Sheet Metal Shop Controls, Kohler and Service Technicians on the job.

Official Opening of Sterling, Virginia office, October 2000: (l to r) H. Thorne Gould, Chairman of the Board; Pat Hurley, General Manager; Clarence W. (Bill) Hottel, Jr., President & CEO; Clarence W. Hottel, Sr., Founder/Chairman Emeritus; Edward E. Fruhling, Vice President Service Operations.

FIDELITY ENGINEERING

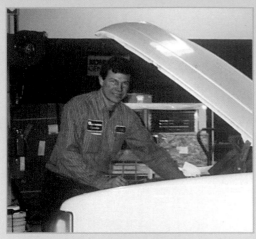

Auto Mechanic Joe McCusker, Jr. maintains all 150 company vehicles (has been with Fidelity for 16 years), 2000.

Joe's helpers: Kyle Palmer and Bill Forster.

Richard Beattie, Vice President, Construction Division.

Jim Slechta, Vice President – Kohler Division (has been with Fidelity for 18 years), 2000.

Company attorney, Thomas J. Schetelich and wife Victoria (center) with Fidility's COB/Treasurer, H. Thorne Gould and wife Hannah, 1997 Christmas Party.

The AMERICAN SOCIETY of REFRIGERATING ENGINEERS

ORGANIZED 1904   INCORPORATED 1906

These are to Certify that

Clarence W. Hottel

is a   Member   of

The American Society of Refrigerating Engineers
an organization for promoting the Arts and Sciences connected with
Refrigeration and for acquiring and perpetuating that Knowledge
which is necessary to the Refrigerating Engineer

Witness our hands and Seal at New York, this
thirty-first day of December 1945.

Charles S. Leopold

1949-1950

ith sincere good wishes for his continued success

this

ertificate of ppreciation

is awarded to

Clarence W. Hottel, Chairman
of the
Baltimore-Washington Section.

he merican ociety of efrigerating ngineers

by his fellow workers, for his faithful services
rendered to this Section.

**American Society of Heating, Refrigerating
and Air-Conditioning Engineers, Inc.**

This is to certify that

Clarence W. Hottel

is a

Life Member

and is entitled to all the rights and privileges
of such membership.

July 1973

Walter F. Spiegel

Certificates indicating Clarence Hottel's membership in the American Society of
Heating, Refrigerating and Air-Conditioning Engineers, Inc. (ASHRAE) since 1945.

FIDELITY ENGINEERING

Fidelity's 50th year celebrated at Annual Company Picnic, 1995.

Thorne Gould and Bill Hottel with Baltimore Oriole Great, Brooks Robinson, at a Company Management Seminar, 1996.

Photos on this page: First company Christmas party at our new location. Children everywhere! 1997.

FIDELITY ENGINEERING RECENT PROJECTS

National Aquarium in Baltimore

Timonium Two Office Building

University of Baltimore

Oriole Park at Camden Yards, Maryland Stadium Authority

Broadmead Center Health Care Facility

Mercantile Bank installation

Alex. Brown, the prestigious investment banking and brokerage firm in Baltimore

Integrated Health Services

HARVEY HOTTEL

Present location of Harvey Hottel, Inc., 18900 Woodfield Road, Gaithersburg, Maryland 20879

Harvey W. Hottel, Inc. at the Baltimore Industrial Show.

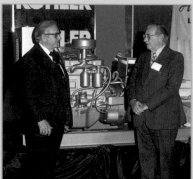

Clarence and Harvey at Kohler Generator Display, Baltimore Industrial Show held at the Baltimore Convention Center, 1982.

Harvey with his son Dick and his family during Christmas 1997 at the Congressional Country Club.

CONTRACTING BUSINESS HALL OF FAME

A PIONEER
IN PERFORMANCE GUARANTEES

Harvey W. Hottel, 1908-1999

When one thinks of performance guarantees in the HVAC industry today, what probably comes to mind is the ability to guarantee a system's performance down to +/- 1 degree of temperature or 2% relative humidity. The fact that the system will work better than, say, a chunk of ice in a box is pretty much taken for granted. But as the saying goes, it didn't always used to be that way.

When Harvey W. Hottel and his twin brother Clarence opened an appliance store in Bethlehem, PA in 1926, they had to find a way to convince grocery store owners to use their new mechanical refrigeration systems instead of the tried-and-true traditional ice delivery service. In the process, they may have pioneered the concept of performance guarantees.

The Hottels told the store owners to try their mechanical refrigerators at the same price that they were paying for ice delivery. If the owners weren't completely satisfied with the new mechanical refrigerators, the Hottels would remove them without further cost, and the owners could go back to their previous service. The Hottels never lost a customer.

A Self-taught Engineer

Harvey W. Hottel was a self-taught engineer who read all the technical literature he could get his hands on and also attended training sessions conducted by industry greats such as Dr. Willis Carrier and Clarence Birdseye. He was eventually awarded a professional engineer's (P.E.) license even though his formal education extended no further than high school.

When the Great Depression forced Harvey and Clarence to close their business in the 1930s, the Hottel brothers went their separate ways. Harvey relocated to Washington, D.C. in the early 1940s, where the Carrier Corporation asked him to establish a refrigeration department to design, install, and guarantee the performance of cold storage systems for the War Department.

As World War II drew to a close, Harvey realized things were about to change dramatically. Up to that time, comfort cooling was simply not available for civilian use, due to war rationing. But he knew people would eagerly embrace this new concept once given a chance to experience it in theaters, restaurants, and offices.

In 1945, Harvey W. Hottel, Inc. was formed. The company began by designing and installing commercial air conditioning systems for government and industrial facilities in the Washington, D.C. area. As his business (and the popularity of air conditioning) grew, Harvey added a service and repair shop. He even developed a manufacturing business by obtaining military contracts for highly specialized air conditioning systems for use in combat equipment. The business continued to expand, and Harvey W. Hottel, Inc. now offers a full range of mechanical and plumbing contracting services to a variety of commercial and residential customers.

As the company prepares to enter the 21st Century, it continues to embrace new technologies, such as geothermal heat pump systems. Harvey W. Hottel, Inc. is a recipient of both a *Quality Home Comfort Award* (July, 1998) and a *Design/Build Award* (December, 1998) from *Contracting Business* for its work with geothermal systems.

The Values of the Founder

Throughout its history, the company that Harvey Hottel founded has always stressed the values of its founder: honesty, hard work, quality workmanship, and responsive service. Harvey's son Richard is now president of the company, and three of his grandsons are working in the business.

Harvey W. Hottel died September 2, 1999, after a bout with cancer. In his passing, he leaves a memorable legacy in the HVACR industry, and *Contracting Business* magazine is proud to help ensure that legacy lives on as we induct him into our Hall of Fame.

Contracting Business Magazine's tribute to Harvey, January 2000.

PRAYER BREAKFAST GROUPS

Dr. Abraham Vereide, Founder of the prayer breakfast movement.

The first Presidential Prayer Breakfast, February 5,1953. (l to r) Abraham Vereide, the Honorable Katharine St. George M.C., and President Eisenhower.

Left to right: Abraham Vereide with President Kennedy, Senator Frank Carlson, Billy Graham, and Vice President Lyndon Johnson following the 1961 Presidential Prayer Breakfast.

Dr. Billy Graham, President Kennedy, and Senator Frank Carlson at the 1961 Presidential Prayer Breakfast.

THE SUN

VOL. 289—NO. 18—E   BALTIMORE, SATURDAY, JUNE 6, 1981

U
ri
in

By Ste
Washingt

Wash
ued to s
tion's un
cent of t
bor Dep
was the
recession

At th
ing indic
tially m
reported
produce
percent
last Dec

Held
wholesal
the May
and a th

The
been st
months,
industry
rates an
the dol
sluggish
and serv

The r
by 425,0
of 8.1 m
had bee
percent
governm
settling
time bei
percent

Total
broad sa
by 260,0
change,
99,235,0

"We

Sun photo—George H. Cook

Morning prayer with Graham

Archbishop Borders, evangelist Billy Graham (center) and Mayor Schaefer joined with 4,000 people in prayer at the Convention Center yesterday morning as Mr. Graham prepared to start an eight-day crusade at Memorial Stadium. During the gathering, the 11th annual

Mayor's Prayer Breakfast, Mr. Graham praised Baltimore's spirit: "I don't know how the Colts and the Orioles ever lose a game. And I hope we win some games this coming week at Memorial Stadium." The breakfast attracted many prominent Maryland politicians. (Article, B1)

The 11th Annual Mayor's Prayer Breakfast In 1981. (l to r) Archbishop Borders, Dr. Billy Graham and Mayor Schaefer. 4,000 were in attendance at the Baltimore Convention Center.

Clarence Hottel and Dr. Billy Graham with faithful volunteer Vera Yancey.

Clarence meets Dr. Grady Wilson and Dr. Alan Streett at the National Prayer Breakfast, Washington, D.C.

PRAYER BREAKFAST GROUPS

National Week of Prayer Luncheon in Baltimore with Joni Eareckson Tada, May 2000.

Bob Gaines, Prison Fellowship Baltimore Director, guest speaker at monthly Prayer Breakfast, also ministers in song.

Faithful pray-ers attend monthly Breakfast Group meetings.

Neil Fichthorn, former President, Sandy Cove Ministries, North East, Maryland.

Everyone singing!

PRAYER BREAKFAST GROUPS

One Voice, special musical guests at a Christmas Breakfast.

Former Baltimore Oriole Pat Kelly is a frequent guest speaker at our monthly Breakfast.

Governor Schaefer (right) chats with Breakfast Group "old timer" Dorwin McDonald.

Dr. Ray Moreland, Executive Director, Maryland Bible Society — annual Breakfast Group guest speaker/soloist.

Corrie ten Boom spoke at one of our Mayor's Prayer breakfasts and a luncheon on the same day to accommodate the large attendance, 1975.

PRAYER BREAKFAST GROUPS

Clarence at Breakfast with Governor Schaefer, May 1999.

Dr. Richard C. Halverson, Chaplain of the United States Senate, June 1981.

Baltimore Breakfast Group Leaders at Clarence's home for an evening of prayer and music, 1998.

Surprise 90th Birthday celebration at Baltimore Breakfast Group with Herbert Fivehouse and Roger Hetzner, 1998.

Baltimore Rescue Mission Executive Director Rev. Charles Buettner (center back row), his wife Janna (left back row) and his family (l to r) Rachel, Stephen and Barbara.

Evie Tornquist at National Prayer Breakfast, Washington, D.C. Clarence Hottel invites her to sing in Baltimore, early 1970s.

Dr. and Mrs. D. James Kennedy on the Coral Ridge Cruise, 1988.

"Faithful John" at Harper House (Clarence's condominium).

Clarence with the Earl W. Schultz, Jr. Family (Youth for Christ/World Outreach Division), November 1991.

Dr. Brett Katzen performed laser cataract surgery on both Harvey and Clarence in 1995.

FRIENDS

Fidelity Engineering, Dunham-Bush Inc., and Harry Hitchcock keep things cool at the Messiah College gymnasium. These three provided and installed the 50-ton air conditioning unit, capable of keeping a crowd of 4,000 people comfortable on a 90-degree day.

Dr. Ray Hostetter turns on the new 50-ton air conditioning unit at Messiah College that was designed and installed by Fidelity Engineering Corporation, 1988.

Harvey and Clarence on Messiah College Scandinavia Tour hosted by Dr. D. Ray and Audrey Hostetter. Group photo taken at Plaza Hotel, Stockholm, Sweden, 1994.

The World of Engineering

About Messiah

As a four-year, coeducational Christian institution, Messiah College offers you an education that is rigorously academic and unapologetically Christian.

That means that you'll share your college experience with other top-notch students, learning together from professors who are experts in their fields as well as caring, committed Christians.

At Messiah, you'll have plenty of opportunities to stretch your mind and nurture your faith. From debating in the classroom to researching in the lab, from giving your all on the playing field to making joyful music in the recital hall, from sharing in the dorm to reaching out in the nearby towns and cities, you're sure to see God working in your life. And when you graduate, you'll be prepared to serve the Lord with excellence in whatever career you choose. Just ask our alumni who are making a difference around the world in every field imaginable.

Founded in 1909, Messiah College is accredited by the Middle States Association of Colleges and Secondary Schools and approved by the Pennsylvania Department of Education.

Our Facilities

Engineering majors will find state-of-the-art technology in Messiah's 65,000-square-foot Frey Hall.

Well-equipped laboratories, sophisticated design and analysis tools, and our professionally staffed model shop help you to excel in your studies. You will also learn to use commercial computer design tools such as Electronics Workbench, Working Model, Lab View, and Algor.

Questions

To get a fun and close-up look at the engineering major at Messiah College, we invite you to participate in our Engineer's Day.

Registration is limited, s____
(717) 766-2511, ext. 2630, f____
To contact our faculty, e-mai____
engineer@messiah.edu. Or v____
web page at http://www.mess____
for a list of employment and ____
school placements of recent ____
engineering graduates.

Student Initiatives

At Messiah College, you'll find plenty of ways to link what you're learning in the classroom with hands-on engineering experience.

You might choose to work on a nationally competitive project like Genesis, Messiah's award-winning solar race car, designed and built by Messiah students. Or you could join the West Africa Outreach team, which is meeting physical and spiritual needs through culturally appropriate technologies and Christian testimony.

Brochure describing Messiah's Engineering department.

Dr. Ray Hostetter and Clarence Hottel with other Messiah friends Mike Shaker (left) and Barry Goodling (right).

FRIENDS

Back to the Bible Week 1999 at Willowbank, Bermuda: (l to r) Dr. Woodrow and Linda Kroll, Clarence Hottel and Dorothy Drinkwater.

Clarence with Bobby Richardson at Fellowship of Christian Athletes Banquet, 1999.

Clarence with Dr. Jerry Falwell, December 1983.

Clarence (in sunglasses) on Dr. Falwell's Holy Land tour 1983.

91st Birthday celebrated at The King's College, Empire State Building in New York City with President Dr. Friedhelm and Elizabeth Radandt, 1999.

DIGITAL STUDIO COMING

Pictured Above: WRBS General Manager Tom Bisset (center) with Clarence Hottel (right) who presented WRBS with check for new digital studio. Dorothy Drinkwater (left).

WRBS' new digital studio will integrate our music programs and satellite feeds into one audio chain. The end result will be super quality audio and greater control over our programming material.*FT*
-*Peter Allen, WRBS Chief Engineer*

Clarence presents Radio Station WRBS-FM General Manager, Tom Bisset, with a check for their new digital studio, 1998.

FRIENDS

United Christian Citizens

Award to

Clarence W. Hottel

— as —

Christian Citizen of the Year 1977

For exemplifying, in all humility, the Christian life and service in the public affairs of the community and your church, serving as President of the Fellowship Foundation, holding weekly Prayer Sessions for the public — a service which aids the spiritual enhancement of the people in our community — and your efforts in initiating and planning the Annual Mayor's Prayer Breakfast.

December 8, 1977

Garrett D. Bailey, President
United Christian Citizens, Inc.

1997 Philanthropic Leadership Award from
Maryland Bible College & Seminary, presented
by its President, Dr. Kent Sutorius.

Christian Citizen of the Year Award, 1977.

Dr. Gilbert Peterson with Richard Wilson presents "Mantle of Stewardship Award" to
Clarence at Lancaster Bible College. Lancaster, PA, 1997.

FRIENDS

Enjoying fellowship at Beachmont Christian Camp with Director Paul Twining and Rev. Les Metcalf, August 1998.

The Clarence W. Hottel, Sr. Learning Center at the Helping Up Mission, Baltimore, Maryland.

Bob and Karon Gehman wedding (Bob is the Executive Director of the Helping Up Mission in Baltimore), December 1999.

J. Stanley Oakes, Jr., President of the International Leadership University.

FRIENDS

Clarence at new property for Hunt Valley Church.

Hunt Valley Church, new building at 13015 Beaver Dam Road, Hunt Valley, MD 21031. Opened in 1998.

Frank Boswell, my Pastor.

Frank and Jeannie Boswell, Jon, Sarah and Lauren (Pastor's family).

Charles Freitag, Sr., Hunt Valley Church "PR" man.

Friends for over 50 years, Herb and Elinor Fivehouse.

Beautiful plaque permanently placed on newly named "Clarence W. Hottel, Sr. Building" at 1031 East Baltimore Street, Baltimore, Maryland.

Charles Hallis, President of Helping Up Mission Board of Directors, read this proclamation at the outdoor ceremony when the plaque was unveiled

Whereas Helping Up Mission has been bringing real hope to the poor and homeless of Baltimore since 1885 through programs that address Physical, Psychological, Social and Spiritual needs; and

Whereas the primary purpose of the Helping Up Mission in serving the needs of the poor and homeless is to honor God and lead all who come to the Helping Up Mission to a personal faith in Jesus Christ; and

Whereas Mr. Clarence W. Hottel, Sr, for many years through his friendship, prayers and financial contributions has been generously supporting this holistic approach to serving the needs of the poor and homeless; and

Whereas the purchase and renovations of the building located at 1031 East Baltimore Street which will be used to serve thousands of Baltimore's needy for years to come was in a large part made possible due to the generosity of Mr. Clarence W. Hottel, Sr.;

We the Helping Up Mission Board of Directors and staff hereby resolve that the 1031 East Baltimore Building on this day March 24, 2001 and from this day forward be named the Clarence W. Hottel, Sr. Building; and may it be further resolved that a plaque honoring the generosity and commitment of Mr. Clarence W. Hottel be permanently placed on the building.

Mr. Charles Hallis
President
Board of Directors

FRIENDS

Jim, Anne, Bill and their families attended the Dedication.

Proud Grandfather – eight of ten grandchildren shared this special day. (Absent: Henry in Georgia and Nancy in California.)

Great GrandDaddy Clarence with (l to r) Devan, Nathaniel, Tiara, Madeleine and Emily.

Congratulations from Executive Director Robert K. Gehman.

Former Governor William Donald Schaefer (now Comptroller of Maryland) presented this Certificate of Recognition at the Dedication Service.

COMPTROLLER
of MARYLAND
Serving the People

Be it hereby known to all that this
Certificate of Recognition
is awarded to

CLARENCE W. HOTTEL, SR.

with congratulations on your illustrious career; with special appreciation for your outstanding leadership, your legendary work ethic, your generous gifts to those in need, and your principled and unselfish spirit; and with my personal best wishes on the splendid occasion of the dedication of the new Hottel building.

Presented this 24th day of March 2001

WILLIAM DONALD SCHAEFER, COMPTROLLER

SHEPHERD COTTAGE

6 Maplewood Road, Lake Harmony

U.S. flag always
flies at Shepherd
Cottage.

Jeff Jones and workers keep the cottage in good shape—both inside and out.

SHEPHERD COTTAGE

Birthday Breakfast in the Poconos (Clarence and Dorothy at favorite restaurant), 1996.

The grandchildren drive our golf cart all around the Split Rock Community.

The Jacuzzi—always a fun place for the grandchildren.

SHEPHERD COTTAGE

The deer are frequent visitors.

Enjoying the sunshine at Lake Harmony beach.

Relaxing in the Poconos with Bob and Carolyn Larson.

Bob Larson and Clarence working together, 1999.

CHAPTER 7

The Cooling Trend Continues

Each thought that is welcomed and recorded is a nest egg,
by the side of which more will be laid.
—Thoreau

H is name was Francois de Salignac de La Mothe Fenelon, a 17th-century Archbishop of Cambrai, France. I had never heard of this spiritual advisor to a small group of earnest Christians at the court of Louis the XIV until my friend Charlie "Tremendous" Jones gave me a copy of the amazing little book *Let Go*. It is a small book indeed—so tiny, in fact, that it could easily be buried by the sheer weight and thickness of the many other tomes in my bookcase. However, in this book's 85 pages are housed some of the most profound truths I have ever read.

In a series of spiritual letters, Fenelon responded to the many queries he received from his faithful flock. Since you may not have a copy of *Let Go* in your library, I would like to share with you Fenelon's Letter 14, simply titled "Pure Faith Sees God Alone." Perhaps its message of hope and power will speak to your heart today.

Fenelon writes,

Do not worry about the future. It makes no sense to worry if God loves you and has taken care of you. However, when God blesses you remember to keep your eyes on Him and not the blessing. Enjoy your blessings day by day just as the Israelites enjoyed their manna, but do not try to store the blessings for the future. There are two peculiar characteristics of pure faith. It sees God behind all the blessings and imperfect

> # The same God who feeds you today is the very God who will feed you tomorrow.

works which tend to conceal Him, and it holds the soul in a state of continued suspense. Faith seems to keep us constantly up in the air, never quite certain of what is going to happen in the future; never quite able to touch a foot to solid ground. But faith is willing to let God act with the most perfect freedom, knowing that we belong to Him and are to be concerned only about being faithful in that which He has given us to do for the moment. This moment by moment dependence, this dark, unseeing peacefulness of the soul under the utter uncertainty of the future, is a true martyrdom which takes place silently and without any stir. It is God's way of bringing a slow death to self. And the end comes so imperceptibly that it is often almost hidden from the sufferer himself, as from those who don't even know he suffers.

Sometimes in this life of faith God will remove His blessings from you. But remember that He knows how and when to replace them, either through the ministry of others or by Himself. He can raise up children from the very stones.

Eat then your daily bread without worrying about tomorrow. There is time enough tomorrow to think about the things tomorrow will bring. The same God who feeds you today is the very God who will feed you tomorrow. God will see to it that manna falls again from Heaven in the midst of the desert, before His children lack any good thing. Francois Fenelon, *Let Go* (Pittsburgh, Pa.: Whitaker House, 1973), pp. 27–28.

While I have always read devotional literature throughout my life, I wish I had known of Fenelon's writings earlier—especially in the early days as we would get call after call asking Fidelity Engineering Corporation to do what often seemed to be the impossible. While I was never a worrywart, there were plenty of times when I know I put more faith in Clarence W. Hottel than in God. As I look back over the years, I can only be grateful to such a merciful, forgiving, loving God who stuck by a young refrigeration engineer who, in his heart, simply wanted to honor his Heavenly Father in all his dealings with clients and family alike. I know He was with me, guiding me and giving our small company the wisdom we needed as we embraced the growing refrigeration industry.

> *I know He was with me, guiding me and giving our small company the wisdom we needed...*

Keeping Theaters Cool . . . and Ice Cream Cold

One day the owner of the nearby Keith Theater called and told me how he was air conditioning his downtown establishment with large, cumbersome, 300-pound cakes of ice that were being hauled into the theater every few days. After spending considerable time at the theater observing an inefficient, costly system of operation, I made the owner an offer I felt he could not refuse: pay my company the same monthly payments he was paying the ice man, and we would install refrigeration to maintain the temperature of the air flow regardless of any change in weather. Further, I promised that as the people "heat load" in the theater changed, the system we designed would

...Fidelity Engineering Corporation became known as the company to do business with.

cut itself off automatically when refrigeration in the airflow was no longer needed. I reminded the theater owner that this design would keep his electric costs to a minimum because of the controlled cooling during each show for both night and daytime loads. The owner took me up on my offer and Fidelity Engineering Corporation was given the contract to install four 25-ton-capacity condensing units with controls that would automatically provide four stages of refrigeration as needed and as called for by the thermostat in the theater. We were getting more and more accounts now as Fidelity Engineering Corporation became known as the company to do business with.

I have often been asked if we installed and serviced ammonia refrigerant installations. The answer is yes. One example is the McCormick Company, where Fidelity Engineering Corporation serviced, replaced, and maintained the ammonia refrigeration system. This operation processed vanilla beans by condensing the liquid in preparation for shipment in large, white enamel drums to large-end users who needed the vanilla seasoning for their products, such as ice cream. We also installed ammonia refrigerant systems in the just-completed cold storage rooms at Mash's Ham Company. We designed ceiling-mounted evaporator coils and interconnected them to remote ammonia compressors. No sooner had we completed one job when the next call came in, and the next, and the next. During one period of Fidelity Engineering Corporation's explosive growth, we equipped the entire original Noxema plant on Falls Road in Baltimore with Carrier products. Not only did we design and install its heating, air conditioning, and ventilation systems, but we also agreed to provide emergency service 24 hours per day. Just as in real estate, where the watchword is location, location, location, in our business we learned early on that service, service, service would be the way not only to survive but to thrive.

> *Herman and Ben were determined to do whatever it would take to produce as good or better signal than their two competitors.*

Heating and Cooling a TV Station

And service is what we also provided from the first day we received a call from Herman and Ben Cohen regarding their purchase of WAAM-TV. The station's antenna was located on top of the 24-story Maryland National Bank building in downtown Baltimore. (The Cohens also had obtained the high hill area near 36th and Falls Road, where they planned to relocate the antenna and construct a building for the station.) Together we went over the preliminary plans, and they asked me to prepare a proposal for all the mechanical heating, air conditioning, and ventilation. It was well known that WAAM had a poor signal and was not able to be competitive with the other two television channels, whose signals were clear.

We called all around to check where new buildings were being constructed exclusively for TV stations, and found that all stations were currently broadcasting from existing tall buildings. Herman and Ben were determined to do whatever it would take to produce as good or better signal than their two competitors. They hired the very best TV technicians, one particularly high-priced key man, and they worked night and day for several years until their signal was as good, or sometimes better, than any of the other stations in this area. I was pleased that Herman and Ben appreciated the way I designed the different zones with separate independent systems to respond to the wide range of varying heat loads, each with its own thermostat control. Some rooms needed considerable heat while some, like the large studio with very hot lights and occasionally large crowds, needed cooling.

> ...Fidelity Engineering Corporation had a continuous replacement and maintenance agreement with the station for service 24 hours a day on all mechanical equipment.

For 25 years, Fidelity Engineering Corporation had a continuous replacement and maintenance agreement with the station for service 24 hours a

Opposite page: This Frigidare mailer from the early 1950s used response cards from Fidelity Engineering's satisfied customers.

THESE CARDS TELL THE
FINAL STORY

day on all mechanical equipment. The managers of many departments were quite demanding, and we learned how to keep the temperature and air conditions the way they liked it. The station's performance became so attractive that Westinghouse bought it from the Cohens, after which it became WJZ-TV (Channel 13).

Finger-Lickin' Good!

One day I received a call from Harvey Kettering, president of the Baltimore Goodwill Industries, who suggested we meet for lunch at the Sheraton Hotel across from Johns Hopkins Hospital. Colonel Sanders, of Kentucky Fried Chicken fame, was scheduled to be the guest speaker at the luncheon. We found his appearance in person to be exactly like the pictures we had seen of him everywhere. He told in his life story how he had lost so many of his customers because a new highway suddenly bypassed his busy little restaurant. That unfortunate turn of events forced him to leave his restaurant, but he knew he had a secret

> *...the Colonel felt something within telling him—due to his upbringing, no doubt—that he owed the Lord's work the tithe money.*

good flavor people liked: a special glazed chicken, better tasting than his competitors. Yes, finger lickin' good! Even though he was broke at around 80 years of age, he took his little old Chevy and, with Social Security as his only income, sold his special formula, which developed, as we all know, into an enormously successful business.

The profits were piling so high that the Colonel felt something within telling him—due to his upbringing, no doubt—that he owed the Lord's work the tithe money. He checked back on the records of his profits and discovered that he owed $600,000. His next problem was to decide which church or organization to give to. Then he said, "There is a man here, and I'll ask him to stand up and verify what happened." It was a colonel from The Salvation Army who said it was true that Colonel Sanders had given that money to The Salvation Army. Colonel Sander's message impressed me immensely, proving again that the words promised in the Book of Malachi come true when we tithe the firstfruits of our income. I thanked my friend Harvey for calling me to join him to hear that motivating message.

> **We were always able to see through the problem to a probable, effective solution.**

Cool 18-Wheelers

In the early days, truck and 18-wheeler trailer manufacturers did not include factory-installed refrigeration systems in their vehicles: ice and dry ice were the only means for cooling. Before long, however, there were increasing demands for dependable low-temperature truck refrigeration systems to haul both normal 40° F produce along with sub-freezing temperature for the transportation of items such as frozen food, ice cream, and orange juice. While we saw most of our assignments as challenges, we were always able to *see through the problem to a probable, effective solution.* That is how our group of Fidelity Engineering Corporation engineers felt when the trucking firm Warner Fruehauf Co., Inc. called and asked us to design and install trailer refrigeration systems.

Fruehauf would construct the bodies of the trucks according to the thickness and type of insulation we specified, after which we would install the

> *This truck refrigeration application was soon able to ship ice cream to Florida and fruit on the return trip back—all in one day, on the same truck.*

necessary refrigeration to operate at the temperature required. Carrier had already designed a special frame we could use to mount a gasoline motor-driven compressor beneath the trailer. Once we connected the compressor to the evaporator cooling coils inside the insulated body, we were ready to run with whatever thermostat-controlled temperature setting might be necessary. This truck refrigeration application proved to be such a success that the Washington Dairy Company was soon able to ship ice cream to Florida and fruit on the return trip back—all in one day, on the same truck. It did not take long for Fruehauf to request an additional nine refrigerated trailers. The orders for refrigerated truck systems to Fidelity Engineering Corporation stopped only when trailer manufacturers began to include refrigeration in their design of new models. It was a good run of business for us for several years.

Speaking of Ice Cream . . .

Along with the Fruehauf success came another similar application with the equipment we installed for the Breyers Ice Cream Company. Its refrigerated trucks brought the frozen ice cream from Philadelphia to a warehouse in Baltimore for quick delivery to the stores. The compressors were sized to provide enough capacity to harden the ice cream properly at -10º F, even when the truck load temperature on hot days was losing several degrees on the road—another satisfied customer with Fidelity installation and service, as is indicated in their letter, still on file in the offices of Fidelity Engineering Corporation.

Our Business Principles Remain the Same

What made our growing enterprise fascinating in the early days of the company is the same thing that makes Fidelity Engineering Corporation the exciting organization it is today: a diversity of clients, a loyal, professional staff, and a wide assortment

> ...a diversity of clients, a loyal, professional staff, and a wide assortment of never-ending business opportunities.

of never-ending business opportunities. As someone once said, "The moment a question comes to your mind, see yourself mentally taking hold of it and disposing of it. In that moment is your choice made. Thus you learn to take the path to the right. Thus you learn to become the decider and not the vacillator. Thus you build character." And, I would add, the development of both a personal and a business character is a never-ending process.

That is how I felt many years ago on the day I received a call from Davidson Chemical Company, a South Baltimore plant that provided refrigeration and dehumidification equipment to ensure the maintenance of a 25 percent relative humidity (R.H.) in silica gel canning—when it was being sealed in cans for the Navy, as specified. We were told that a Navy officer would appear regularly and open a can to test the R.H. before it was shipped. If it tested over 25 percent R.H., he would refuse to ship it. This dilemma made us scratch our heads for some time before we came up with an innovative solution.

> *...the assembly line machinery required so much refrigeration that it would have been too cold for people to work there.*

The facility itself was an old, leaky building with loose doors, windows in various stages of disrepair, and no insulation. Outside design conditions were 95º F and 80 percent R.H. This was before calculating the product load of filled cans coming down the line to be sealed at 25 percent R.H. The Navy's rush priority for this refrigeration application did not provide time for construction work. Therefore, we were forced to make a safe load estimate. It was the best we could do given the circumstances. The high induction load, lights, employees, silica gel product load in cans, and the assembly line machinery required so much refrigeration that it would have been too cold for people to work there.

We solved the problem with a large Carrier-made industrial dehumidifier with gas-fired heat to dry a large, rotating drum of silica gel. Our task was to heat the building to offset the cold refrigeration air to 65º F room temperature, while the humidistat controlling the refrigeration compressor was set to keep the compressors running until the room humidity was under 25 percent R.H. The project was a success, and there were no U.S. Navy rejections.

Working through Discouragement

As I sit at my desk writing these words, I find myself amazed not only at the tremendous opportunities we received daily to do innovative, creative engineering, but also at the great cooperation we received continually from all sides. On one occasion while installing a walk-in cooler with a freezer section for Percy Crawford's Christian Camp at Pinebrook, we found upon start-up that the compressor had a broken connecting rod. In desperation we called the Carrier branch in New Jersey (the Brunswick Kroshell plant), from which it had been shipped. We told the people there of our awful predicament, emphasizing that a large truckload of fresh meat and perishables was on the way to Pinebrook from Philadelphia to be stored in the walk-in cooler we were installing. I'll never forget how Carrier sent a man in a pickup truck with the necessary parts to help us get the compressor running in time to save the food from spoiling on that hot, humid day. Because Percy Crawford's camp was such a vital ministry to our young people—and an organization I have supported from its beginnings—I will forever be in debt to Carrier and its representative who helped save the day by responding to our urgent call.

Rev. Percy Crawford, my dear friend and founder of King's College. His camp was a vital ministry to our young people.

Something else will stick in my mind. When the repairman had completed his work, he shook my hand, smiled, and said, "There will be no charge!" From that moment on, through Fidelity Engineering Corporation and Harvey W. Hottel, Inc., the Hottel twin brothers sold, installed, and serviced many millions of dollars worth of Carrier equipment in the Baltimore/Washington, D.C., area and were blessed in the following years by becoming leaders in our industry.

I must admit there were times when the going was tough, particularly for my family during the years Jack was ill and especially just before he died. I confess there were days when Dottie and I almost felt like giving up. But we knew that successful people keep moving; they don't quit! We knew we neither could nor should jump ship, regardless of how difficult it might be to carry on. So we made the decision to continue to service our customers' accounts diligently 24 hours a day, when new sales were down and strong, aggressive competition seemed to rear its head wherever we looked at an increasingly gloomy horizon. It was all very discouraging. I have always thanked God that Dottie stuck with me—while all the time she did her best to keep the children reasonably happy, although they never fully knew what we were going through at the time.

> **I confess there were days when Dottie and I almost felt like giving up.**

As Anne, Jack, Bill, and Jim grew up in the center of rushing, night-and-day activity, Bill and Jim seemed to take to the business automatically. However, major challenges and obstacles still faced us. Today, when I hear my friends say they hope their children do not have to experience the hardships they went through, I find myself disagreeing with them. Those tough times made us what we are today. I have always believed that a person can be disadvantaged in many ways—one of which is not having to struggle. Suddenly, with our boys' growing interest in developing the business, overnight we were blessed with "four owners" hard at work. No longer was it Dottie and I laboring alone. Bill and Jim jumped in and ran service calls night and day.

Our expanded family enterprise soon led to the next huge step of faith. In 1972, with much prayer, good planning, and hard work, we moved the company to the new Hunt Valley Industrial Park. We gradually became recognized

Jim (left) and Bill (right) took to the business automatically. No longer were Dottie (center) and I laboring alone. Date 1964.

as leaders in the art of designing and building highly specialized computer rooms for the new generation of large computers needed by giant companies. This led to the necessity of tying in to a large Carrier-recommended computer system, which Dottie considered to be a world apart from her trusty manual accounting system—a series of technical innovations that would require extensive training both at home and in Ohio. Now, with a rapidly expanding refrigeration business, Dottie felt any additional technical training would be too much for her to undertake. She had the foresight to see the writing on the wall that clearly suggested Fidelity Engineering Corporation hire an experienced controller and CPA, since our company was on the verge of making an exponential leap into a new era. She also made the wise decision to step aside from the day-to-day activities, but

> **Our company was on the verge of making an exponential leap into a new era.**

kept in touch with the operation. She left our sons and me a solid foundation on which to expand our enterprise. Therefore, we entered a new world of business and unparalleled opportunity.

Blessed with a productive past, and working diligently to enjoy a successful present, we pressed ahead with a belief in our hearts that the future would be even better. We have not been disappointed. God chose to bless our sincere and honest efforts.

Over 50 Years of Excellence

F IDELITY ENGINEERING *Corporation*

AIR CONDITIONING • REFRIGERATION • VENTILATING • HEATING
CONTROLS • PLUMBING • KOHLER GENERATORS
24 Hour Emergency Service
410-771-9400   800-787-6000

Almost daily wherever we go someone tells us they have just seen one of our 150 trucks go by!

TRUE STATEMENT: The Hottel Twins designed and installed many Carrier applications of refrigeration, starting 75 years ago.

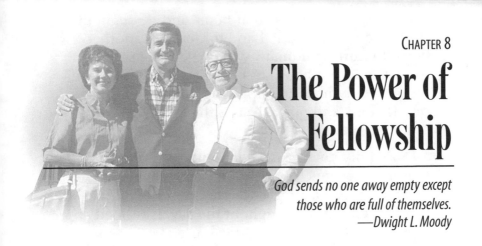

CHAPTER 8

The Power of Fellowship

*God sends no one away empty except
those who are full of themselves.*
—*Dwight L. Moody*

I n the 1880s a young man who was an earnest
Christian found employment in a pawnshop.
Although he disliked the work, he did it faithfully "as unto the Lord" until a more desirable opportunity opened for him. To prepare himself for a life
of Christian service, he wrote on a scrap of paper
the following resolutions: "I do promise God that I
will rise early every morning to have a few minutes—not less than five—in private prayer. I will
endeavor to conduct myself as a humble, meek,
and zealous follower of Jesus, and by serious witness and warning I will try to lead others to think
of the needs of their immortal souls. I hereby vow
to read no less than four chapters in God's Word
every day. I will cultivate a spirit of self-denial and
will yield myself a prisoner of love to the Redeemer
of the world." That young man was William Booth,
founder of The Salvation Army. It is common
knowledge that The Army continues to have an

enormous influence both at home and throughout the world as it lifts one hand to God and another down to hurting humanity. However, The Salvation Army would not be what it is today had it not been for one godly man who took the time to get down on his knees and pray. That is the ultimate source of power!

During my youth as a Mennonite pastor's son, prayer was as much a part of my active life as breath itself. As a family, we prayed in the morning, at night, and throughout the day. It seemed that all we did was pray. Often our prayers were long; sometimes short. However, whenever I prayed—and this is true for as long as I can remember—I always knew that God was by my side listening to my praise, my complaints, and my many requests. I knew I believed in a God who cared about me and loved me no matter how unfaithful I may have been to Him—and I failed Him often. My primary obligation to the God I loved was simply that I must come to Him daily in humble prayer and meet the conditions of God's Word, our daily manual.

> **"Dear God, Your will, nothing more, nothing less, nothing else. Amen."**

A Movement Begins

At a meeting of the Fellowship of Christian Athletes some time ago, Bobby Richardson, former second baseman for the New York Yankees, offered a prayer that is a classic in its brevity and poignancy. He prayed, "Dear God, Your will, nothing more,

The first Presidential Prayer Breakfast at the Mayflower Hotel in Washington, February 5, 1953. Left to right: Abraham Vereide, the Honorable Katharine St. George M.C., President Eisenhower, Senator Carlson (President of International Christian Leadership International), and Conrad Hilton, the host of the breakfast.

nothing less, nothing else. Amen." In those 11 words, Bobby gave us the ultimate reason for praying: *it is all about God's will.* I think I am beginning to understand this now as I grow into a deeper understanding of the power of prayer. Over the years as this awareness slowly overtook me, I began to see a profound need to join hands with others for whom prayer was also a vital part of their lives.

You can imagine my joy when I was invited to attend the first Presidential National Prayer Breakfast at the Mayflower Hotel in Washington, D.C., on February 5, 1953. At that historic event, Norwegian immigrant Abraham Vereide's years of dreams and prayers for a prayer breakfast movement in this country made their initial impact. President Eisenhower and Billy Graham were the two principal speakers. The Word of God was declared, and testimonies rang throughout the ballroom, which was filled to capacity. Senator Frank Carlson presided and Conrad Hilton was our host (he also paid for the breakfast). Jerome Hines, with his tremendous voice, sang several familiar hymns of the faith, after which he gave his own inspiring testimony of how he had found faith and wholeness in Jesus Christ.

Several of my colleagues from Baltimore and I left that great breakfast meeting inspired and determined to throw our support behind the Baltimore Prayer Breakfast Group. Further, we made a commitment to plan an Annual Mayor's Prayer Breakfast, which would be patterned after the National Presidential program. It did not take us long to organize ourselves. Within days, we invited Dr. Richard Halverson, who later became chaplain of the U.S. Senate, to be our guest speaker for the first Baltimore Mayor's Prayer Breakfast. It was the beginning of an annual event that has continued uninterrupted every year since, and has now expanded to include a Governor's Prayer Breakfast—both of which have grown to be among the largest such events in the country. When Corrie ten Boom was once our guest speaker, we were obliged to have her repeat her inspiring message at a luncheon in the Hilton to accommodate the overflow crowd. Later, Dr. Billy Graham drew an audience of more than 4,000 when he addressed our group at the Baltimore Convention Center. I can honestly say that I have been enthusiastic about the impact of our breakfast movement on thousands of people's lives as I have been about the continued growth and success of

> **It was the beginning of an annual event that has continued uninterrupted every year since...**

Fidelity Engineering Corporation. Our Baltimore Group has now met for more than 46 years, and only God knows the number of lives that have been touched by the hundreds of inspiring speakers we have heard during those years. These days I find myself closing my eyes with prayerful thanks that God has given me the privilege of being one of His trusted stewards to help encourage others who are working and studying for the cause of Christ and His Kingdom.

People often ask me how the prayer breakfast movement got its start. Whose idea was it? Who provided the original impetus, and what are the goals of the movement today? Rather than try to speak on behalf of the founder of the modern breakfast movement, my friend Dr. Vereide, I want you to hear from his own pen about the genesis and goals of what is today one of the most influential Christian movements throughout the world. Dr. Vereide writes,

Dr. Abraham Vereide,
Founder of the prayer breakfast movement.

It was by the Sea of Tiberias, more than 1,900 years ago, that the Breakfast Groups had their start. Businessmen and workers at their trade had a meeting with Jesus. That morning, they received instruction in how to do their business. They found an enriching fellowship,

*physical warmth, and a new challenge for life
(John 21).*

*The birth of the Breakfast Groups in this later era
began with a meeting of business executives in Seattle,
Washington, in April of 1935. They were gathered
together to face a critical situation existing in the life of
their city. As they continued in their weekly meetings,
there was born a new vision of a life of usefulness. A
new purpose for living
was recognized, that
of being agents of
God's plan in person-
al, business, and com-
munity life. New pow-
er came as men
believed and obeyed
God.*

> *The transformation
> of men brought
> transformation into
> home, business, and
> government.*

*The contagion of
the new life resulted
in the establishment of groups in shops, homes, the
church, schools, and clubs. Men shared their experience
and translated theory into action, thus producing Christian leadership by precept and example. Members
turned business trips into missionary opportunities, and
the politician became the ambassador of Christ and the
labor leader a minister of reconciliation. The group
became a team for action. The transformation of men
brought transformation into home, business, and government.*

*The idea spread across the continent, and soon Break-
fast Groups sprang up in Chicago, Boston, Philadelphia, and Washington. As the idea caught fire, leaders
in many walks of life came together searching for the
answer to their problems. Today men of varying religious, economic, and cultural backgrounds are meeting*

to plan, pray, and work together. Weekly meetings are held by members of the United States Senate, House of Representatives, departments of the U.S. Government, state and municipal governments, and men from offices and factories. Similar groups have been started amongst women. Campus groups for students and faculties have also been established.

In other countries people have seen new hope through men united for Christian action and in a common faith and devotion to Jesus Christ. In 1947 an international conference was held in Zurich, Switzerland, with representatives from the U.S. Congress and leaders from other walks of life in the U.S. and Europe. Since that time, a world conference has been held every two years in Europe. International Christian Leadership (ICL) groups are now established in over forty countries and are rapidly spreading throughout every continent.

I thought often about Abraham Vereide's words regarding the first "breakfast group" held there on the shores of the Sea of Tiberias so long ago...

Throughout the world, men in business, industry, labor, education, and the professions, as well as men in government at every level are finding understanding, confidence, and hope for the future in the expanding Kingdom of God and in the climate of human relations that Jesus Christ makes possible. Successful global cooperation becomes practical and inevitable as the teachings of Jesus Christ are known and practiced.[1]

---

[1] Dr. Abraham Vereide, Breakfast Luncheon and Fireside Groups Handbook (Washington, D.C.: International Christian Leadership, n.d.), foreword.

It was a peak event in my life when, in December 1971, I had the privilege of attending the Jerusalem Conference on Biblical Prophecy. To spend a week in the Holy Land with some of the giants of the faith was truly one of the greatest thrills of my life. You can be sure I thought often about Abraham Vereide's words regarding the first "breakfast group" held there on the shores of the Sea of Tiberias so long ago—where I, too, was privileged to stand.

As I think of my friend Abraham, I also am reminded of others who helped me in my life's direction. These would include Douglas Coe, who worked closely with Dr. Vereide, and Dr. Richard Halverson. These two men carefully controlled the plans and programs and directed the deliberations of the International Christian Leadership annual

His workload was taking its toll as he began feeling physically and spiritually exhausted to the point of utter despair.

National Presidential Prayer Breakfast. These God-honoring events have always been run first class in every detail, without Doug or Dick demanding any prominence—or even sitting at the head table. I learned from Doug Coe, for the most part, how to conduct our Baltimore Breakfast Group in a manner similar to the operation of the National Prayer Breakfast in Washington, D.C.

Lives Changed through Fellowship

While the weekly fellowship with like-minded Christian men and women was continually charging my spiritual batteries, the breakfasts were also becoming a *must-attend occasion* for hundreds of others throughout Baltimore. I will never forget a man named Harry Hitchcock who arrived at one of our meetings early one morning. Harry was a workaholic, admitting that he was willing to do just about anything that was legal to get ahead in his company. However, his workload was taking its toll as he began feeling physically and spiritually exhausted to the point of utter despair.

One day a friendly neighbor, Frank Mitchell, invited an overworked, underappreciated Harry to our breakfast group meeting in the Pine Room at the Belvedere Hotel. When we met Harry for the first time, we welcomed him enthusiastically with the "right hand of fellowship." I do not think he was accustomed to the robust, early-morning gusto that came from the sincere hearts of his peers. It did not take long, however, for him to feel comfortable with us as he

Clarence Hottel celebrating Harry Hitchcock's 90th birthday in 1987. Harry was a Christian philanthropist who gave of his wealth to many non-profit organizations— schools, colleges, churches, foreign missions—and for the needs of the poor.

warmed to the men in the fellowship—people he felt he could trust. Within a short time, he made our Friday morning fellowship meetings a top priority. Harry confided to the group that the deep longing in his heart was not being satisfied with material things or simply making more money. He told us he wanted something more—as we all did—and that what he really wanted was a deep, inner peace for his troubled heart. Because he was now being exposed to regular Bible teaching, Christian love, and the genuine warmth of other businessmen, Harry made the decision to believe God's Word *no matter what the cost,* just as other businessmen were doing in breakfast groups throughout the country. It did not take Harry long to put his heart on the line and make a sincere commitment to follow his Savior and Lord. He became a very close friend to me for more than 35 years. Regularly, we went together to the annual National Presidential Prayer Breakfast in Washington, D.C., which he so enjoyed and to which he made substantial donations over the years. He told us he had decided to make Christ preeminent in his life so that he might become a worthy ambassador of the Lord he now loved.

BECAUSE OF HIS DECISION, HARRY WAS NEVER THE SAME.

Because of his decision, Harry was never the same. His life was changed and his priorities were rearranged. His motto for the many years that followed was "All to His Honor and Glory." Harry was just one of thousands of men who saw a spiritual need in his life and decided to do something about it—by joining a group of fellow strugglers who were intent on knowing God through His Word and Christian fellowship. Harry moved to Lancaster and later became president of the Lancaster Prayer Breakfast Group, where he served faithfully for more than 30 years, in addition to being president of his company. Harry was a Christian philanthropist who gave of his wealth to many non-profit organizations—schools, colleges, churches, foreign missions—and for the needs of the poor.

Breakfast in the Poconos

A heating and air conditioning contractor in Mount Pocono, Pennsylvania, knew of our Baltimore Breakfast Group ministry and mentioned it to Jack Kalins, president of Split Rock Resort. Mr. Kalins contacted me, suggesting that we have such a meeting at Split Rock in the galleria, which was a new convention center under construction—with a dining room to accommodate 1,500 people.

While this still has not happened, he asked if we would consider conducting the Annual Holy Week service at his church, taking charge of the meeting as we would conduct our weekly breakfasts in Baltimore. We arranged a simple program and advised Mr. Kalins we would be at the Mount Pocono Methodist Church at 7:30 a.m., agreeing to conduct the service for their annual Men's Holy Week service/breakfast. When we arrived, Mr. Kalins was at the entrance to welcome us and lead us to the platform. We looked out over the auditorium and saw there were 250 men attending the service, which we learned later is an important occasion each year for them.

The program consisted of my explanation of the breakfast group idea and how it has grown throughout the world. We then introduced Mary Ellen Criste, who sang several beautiful songs, after which Bert Criste gave a testimony of what the Lord had done for him

Our example, good or bad, leaves an indelible impression on those around us.

in his life. Following that, Rev. Robert Gehman was introduced—a man well prepared to give a gospel message from God's Word. The meeting closed with a prayer and hymn. Many came up to thank us for coming. We then went down to the basement and enjoyed a good breakfast—another powerful example of the great demand for Christian fellowship in a world that is going at breakneck speed.

You Are Making an Indelible Impression

Years ago the communist government in China commissioned an author to write a biography of Hudson Taylor with the purpose of distorting the facts and presenting him in a bad light. They wanted to discredit the name of this consecrated missionary of the gospel. As the author was doing his research, Taylor's saintly character and godly life increasingly impressed him, and he found it extremely difficult to carry out his assigned task with a clear conscience. Eventually, at the risk of losing his life, he laid aside his pen, renounced his atheism, and asked Jesus to become his Lord. The physical results of his decision were painful, but the spiritual rewards he received for his unflinching decision prepared him for eternity.

I think it is important to take note of the deeper meaning of this story. For whether we realize it or not, our example, good or bad, leaves an indelible impression on those around us. That is why I remain committed to our Baltimore Breakfast Group, a fellowship that has been part of my personal and business life for more than 46 years. The purpose of our group has always been to create an environment whereby Jesus Christ can leave an indelible impression on a person's heart. Then through heartfelt fellowship with all who attend, we have the privilege to be there when we need each other both in times of joy and sorrow.

I have often heard it said that *truth is indivisible.* Either something is true, or it is not. It is right, or it is not. I would agree. That is why I have always had great joy in being a follower of Christ at home, at leisure, or in the office *because the hope Christ gives must be in evidence everywhere*—in both the secular and religious arenas of life. For example, at Fidelity Engineering Corporation, I want my influence to

> I want my influence to inspire our younger generation to excel in engineering, to demonstrate unquestioned integrity, and not to be just as good as but to be better than the competition.

inspire our younger generation to excel in engineering, to demonstrate unquestioned integrity, and not to be just as good as but *to be better than the competition.* I want our staff of engineers and their associates to be more prompt in their response to our customers' needs, to be better prepared for the inevitable emergencies of our clients, to be more faithful in their daily tasks, to be more dependable, more honest,

> *We, too, must maintain a balance that will keep our work and service in a kind of creative tension. Not to do so is a formula for burnout.*

and to be known as the kinds of *promise keepers* who treat every call that comes in as if it were a drop of gold.

I have discovered in more than 60 years of designing and selling the latest kinds of technical equipment in our field that these are the qualities our clients, buyers, and customers are looking for. Fidelity Engineering Corporation has built its reputation on that firm foundation, and I want the new generation to take our success to the next critical level without ever forgetting the qualities that make for true success. Without question the job of our organization is to provide the finest research, the best service, and the most efficient, cost-effective, state-of-the-art refrigeration, heating, and generators in the industry to our customers. However, if that is *all* we are, it will never be enough. Just as an airplane must have two wings that are balanced if it is to fly safely, so we, too, must maintain a balance that will keep our work and service in a kind of creative tension. *Not to do so is a formula for burnout.* Both quiet times for personal introspection and meaningful activities that take us beyond ourselves and our own challenges promise to enhance our emotional and spiritual well-being.

Messiah College

During the early 1980s, at an International Christian Leadership Banquet in Washington, D.C., we met a beautiful young couple, Mark and Jeannie, who were just graduated from Messiah College in Grantham, Pennsylvania. They radiated their love for the Lord and thrilled to tell their highest praise and appreciation for what they had learned at their alma mater. Their fine Christian spirit spoke volumes that impressed me about the college. I discussed this with my friend Harry Hitchcock, who had just recently been a substantial donor to help build a large gymnasium at Messiah. The gym was not air-conditioned, so Fidelity Engineering Corporation submitted a proposal, which the Board accepted. The air conditioning was installed before the next graduation, when 4,000 were in attendance.

Dr. Ray Hostetter turns on the new 50-ton air conditioning unit at Messiah College that was designed and installed by Fidelity Engineering Corporation. Date 1988.

The president, Dr. Ray Hostetter, gave me a book, *Messiah College: A History.* From this I learned that my origin was close to the Brethren in Christ founders of Messiah College, which made me feel safe to consider being one of their donors to help Dr. Hostetter fulfill his dream of adding engineering and business to their curriculum.

I have been hiring people for more than 60 years, looking for people who are sound, born-again Christians, professional graduates in our technical engineering field, and who have a graduate degree in business. These are the kind of people I believe Messiah can produce; we want their applications now, and upon graduation there will be good jobs waiting for them.

Reprint of Engineering Newsletter, October 1999

■ The Engineering Department is pleased to announce the creation of a rotating scholarship chair, endowed by a gift from Mr. Clarence Hottel of Fidelity Engineering in Baltimore, Md. Mr. Hottel is a longtime friend of the department and member of the advisory board that began Messiah's BSE program. Thanks to his gift, members of the Engineering faculty may apply for release time in support of a scholarship project. The endowment provides each recipient of the Hottel Chair with release time equivalent to one semester, to be distributed over the course of a two-year appointment. The endowment also provides to each recipient a research grant.

Dr. David Vader has been appointed the first Hottel Chair of Engineering. For several years, the Engineering professors and staff have experimented with service learning as a means of influencing our graduates toward more responsible engineering. Creating and using technology may indeed, as Samuel Flormen suggests[1], provide existential pleasures for the engineer. Technology, however, is what philosophers call an instrument value[2]. It is not valuable itself, but is valuable because it enables one to achieve something else that is valuable. In his application for the Hottel Chair, Dr. Vader proposes that an engineer discovers the inherent value in her or his work when engineering is practiced as a kind of service.

Engineering

- Engineering
  Mechanical Concentration
  Electrical Concentration
- Civil Engineering

MESSIAH COLLEGE

Our Program

At Messiah College, you'll find studying engineering is an exciting challenge. But it's much more than just learning the skills to become a successful engineer. As a Messiah engineering graduate, you'll be technically competent, broadly educated, and nurtured in character and conduct consistent with the commitments of our Christian faith.

In addition to knowledge in the liberal arts, you'll gain a thorough grounding in engineering fundamentals to prepare you for lifelong learning. Through your studies, you'll learn to "see the big picture," ask important questions, and learn on your own. You'll also learn by doing as well as knowing, with course projects that take you beyond the classroom to apply theory to contemporary engineering problems and real-world design. A number of local companies and global service organizations often help define and sponsor student work, helping you learn to adapt materials and energy to meet the physical needs of people and care for God's creation.

As a Messiah engineer, you'll be prepared for both leadership and servanthood, gaining skills in technical and commercial concerns while learning to value social, political, cultural, environmental, economic, and human empowerment issues.

Our Faculty

As an engineering major, you will enjoy studying with caring Christian faculty who are academically qualified and eager to share both teaching and industry experience with students.

Most importantly, each faculty member has experienced God's call to ministry through teaching at Messiah College.

Small class sizes offer you plenty of opportunity for one-on-one support and interaction. Special projects enable you to work side by side with professors, learning and growing together. And don't be surprised to see your profs cheering you on in extracurricular activities or joining you for a bite to eat in the snack shop. They really want to get to know you as an individual and help you reach your full potential.

Our Graduates

Messiah's BSE program gives you excellent preparation for graduate school.

However, our graduates have received a solid base for entering the work force immediately.

Electrical Concentration: As we enter a new millennium, rapid technological advances in electrical engineering have created excellent employment opportunities for electrical engineers. From communications, electronic controls, and digital circuit design to service-oriented work in small-scale power generation, print

and non-print media, and new computer applications, our graduates are serving God in a diverse range of fields.

Mechanical Concentration: Messiah graduates concentrating in mechanical engineering have chosen from a rich variety of career paths, including mechanical component and system design, energy conversion and power production, and industrial and manufacturing engineering, as well as computer-aided design and manufacturing. Service opportunities include small-scale manufacturing, transportation, and agricultural processing.

Dual Concentration: With an extra semester or a few summer classes, some of our students choose to pursue a double concentration, enabling them to practice interdisciplinary engineering.

Civil Engineering Degree: After spending their last four semesters at Messiah's Philadelphia Campus, our civil engineering graduates find employment in the fields of construction, water resources, traffic control, and land development. Focusing on developing products that safely serve people, some civil engineers work outdoors, while others perform their jobs in a more typical office environment.

Accreditation

Offered with concentrations in electrical and mechanical engineering, Messiah's Bachelor of Science in Engineering (BSE) degree is accredited by the Engineering Accreditation Commission (EAC) of the Accreditation Board for Engineering and Technology (ABET).

The degree in civil engineering (BSCE) is offered through studying two years at Messiah's Philadelphia Campus in conjunction with Temple University. The civil engineering degree is not ABET accredited.

A Christian college of the liberal and applied arts and sciences.

Among the many reasons we made this rotating scholarship available to engineering students at Messiah College are the following:

■ **We need youthful enthusiasm for the engineering tasks that lie ahead.**

■ **We want students who will read and study, be honest, trustworthy, and live lives of integrity.**

■ **We need people committed to *excellence in engineering,* with a graduate college degree in mechanical and electrical contractions and a course in business.**

■ **We want Christian-principled engineers— the type of employees always preferred by Fidelity Engineering Corporation and most employers.**

■ **We need the kind of student who will be worthy of good pay, who is a quick study, and who quickly learns how to serve others better than the competition.**

■ **We need a student who will naturally become a leader with his or her company, thus enhancing the opportunity to become part of company management.**

Two cases in point: The delivery man and truck driver who delivered my solid mahogany desk more than 50 years ago became president of Baltimore Stationery Company. When he passed away, his wife became chairman of the board.

One of the largest Chevrolet dealers in Baltimore—Anderson Chevrolet—is now owned and managed by Bruce Mortimer, a faithful and dependable top salesman who worked hard and successfully for Mr. Anderson for many years.

Ideas are a dime a dozen, but *people who can put them into action are priceless.* Through meaningful philanthropy, we will continue to put our dollars into those with eager minds and receptive hearts—such as we have done with our gift to Messiah College.

I am so confident of the necessity of this philanthropic approach for an abundant life that we have set up a Christian Gift Annuity Fund, from which we have already given more than $2.5 million to help support schools, colleges, churches, camps, radio and television programs, and rescue missions. Recently, we gave 7,000 copies of the Contemporary English Version of *Year of the Bible* free of charge to schools and colleges. The thousands of good customers who have purchased their air conditioning and generators from Fidelity Engineering Corporation over the years have made these donor funds possible—helping countless numbers of men and women know that there is hope in a confusing, often disheartening world—for which we say *thank you.*

> **WE WERE NOT MEANT TO LIVE IN ISOLATION BUT RATHER IN COMMUNITY.**

We Need Each Other

Several years ago studies were conducted among former American prisoners of war to determine what methods used by the enemy had been most effective in breaking their spirit. The findings revealed that they did not break down from physical deprivation and torture as quickly as they did from solitary confinement or from disrupted friendships caused by frequent changing of personnel. Attempts to get the prisoners divided in their attitudes toward one another proved to be the most successful method of discouraging them. It was further learned that the soldiers were not sustained primarily by faith in their country or by the rightness of the cause for which they fought. They drew their greatest strength from the close attachments they had formed to the small military units to which they belonged.

What can we learn from these observations? Essentially, that we need each other. We need each other's friendship, counsel, and fellowship— whether it is a prayer breakfast group or conversation over a cup of coffee with an understanding neighbor. We were not meant to live in isolation but rather in community. This is what I am learning as I look back on my life. The most important moments for me have been those I have spent in

> *Being in the "joy of God's presence" is one of the elements that makes miracles happen.*

prayer and conversation with family and colleagues I love and respect. Now as I review the inner richness of my more than 91 years, I give all thanks to God for whatever success may have come my way. I also continue to pray along with Andrew Murray, a Christian from another era who continues to touch millions through his devotional writings: *May not a single moment of my life be spent outside the light, love, and joy of God's presence and not a moment without the entire surrender of myself as a vessel for Him to fill full of His Spirit and His love.*

Miracles Abound

Being in the "joy of God's presence" is one of the elements that makes miracles happen. As I write those words, my mind wanders back to some miraculous incidents that happened to me. One night, while driving home from a series of ASHRAE meetings in Trenton, New Jersey, about eleven o'clock, I fell asleep. The

> **The bright colors of the window curtains got my attention when it dawned on me:** *Could the house possibly be on fire?*

bump and noise as my car drifted off the paved road woke me up, and I saw a tree like it was coming fast toward me. I turned the steering wheel hard to the right and missed the tree, except for a knock on the side of my door. When I stopped to check, I found that the door handle was torn off, which is an indication of how close I was to having been possibly killed. I thanked the Lord all the way home that I was alive.

I then remember another time when I believe the Lord was truly standing before me, protecting me in every way. It was late and bitter cold when I left Bethlehem, on my way to Reading to be with my folks for the weekend, when I passed a single house on my left. It looked strangely lighted against the background of a dark field. The bright colors of the window curtains got my attention when it dawned on me: *Could the house possibly be on fire?*

After driving a couple miles, I decided to turn around and go back to make certain. Sure enough, the curtains and the whole living room were on fire, and there was no sign of anyone moving about in the house. I blew my horn and directed my bright lights on the house and threw stones at the second-floor windows. This woke up the occupants. Immediately, an elderly couple and a lady with two children and a baby came rushing down a stairway off the living room, all in their nightclothes and bare footed. I put them in my heated car. There were no other houses nearby, but a house suddenly lit up on the other side of the highway. I took the baby to this only house available, and the woman who lived there said as she took the baby, "We have not spoken for years." I then took the family to the county firehouse, where they would be warm and cared for. The next morning, the Reading morning newspaper ran an article with the headline, AN UNKNOWN TOURIST SAVED THE LIVES OF A FAMILY.

> *I believe it was the prompting of God's angels or the Holy Spirit who guided me to make the decision to turn around and go back.*

I did not know them, and they did not know me. The good news is that the people were saved, even though their home had burned to the ground. I believe it was the prompting of God's angels or the Holy Spirit who guided me to make the decision to turn around and go back. Many times over the following years, I thought about these people as I passed by between Allentown and Reading, wondering how they made out, and what they said to their neighbors when they came to get their baby.

Looking back and remembering experiences such as this encourages me to obey the prompting of the Holy Spirit instead of ignoring the urge to "drive by" because it is too late and too cold. I wanted to get home and get comfortable. If the morning newspaper had run a picture of a burned-down house and told of a family that had perished in the flames, then how would I have felt, and how much of the blame for the death of those people might have been on me?

Almost Missed It!

If you have ever been on a cruise, you know what a delightful experience it can be—especially when the pressures of modern life come down with a vengeance and you simply need to get away for few days. Well, let me tell you about how I almost missed my cruise of a lifetime. Through correspondence, and having enjoyed the company of Dr. D. James Kennedy as the guest speaker at our Maryland Governor's Prayer Breakfast, the well-known pastor and I became good friends. One day he insisted that I go along on his next cruise to Nassau, even though the cabins had all been sold. He said there is always a last-minute cancellation and I could count on a good cabin. I believe he knew of such a vacancy, so I agreed to go. The SS *Emerald Seas* was scheduled to leave Miami on a Monday, so I took a flight on Saturday to Fort Lauderdale in order to attend worship with Dr. Kennedy at the Coral Ridge Presbyterian Church.

I rented a car at the airport and checked into a hotel near the church. Saturday night I attended a wonderful musical concert and then enjoyed the Sunday morning and evening services. Dr. Kennedy invited me to go directly from the church to the ship (which I should have done). I told him that I had a rental car I could drive to Miami and leave there, and then board the ship.

Monday morning I left the hotel in good time, but when I arrived in Miami, I was not able to find the National Car Rental place to leave the car. I called National's office where I rented the car, and I was given an address in Miami where I could drop it off. I roamed all over, asking people for its location, but for the life of me I could not find a National Car Rental agency anywhere near the address I had been given. In desperation I found a public telephone and called them back. They gave me another address, saying they were sorry they had given me a wrong address earlier. They told me to try a certain place; I roamed throughout the entire area and still found no place to leave the car.

Time was now my enemy...

Time was now my enemy, as I began to fear that I might miss boarding the ship. In desperation, I stopped my car on a busy street, walked toward a policeman, and talked him into my leaving the car in a no-parking zone while I went across the street to a high-rise office building to find a public phone and tell the National people I was simply going to leave the car where it was and hail a taxi to the ship. I promised the police officer that I would move the car from where I had parked it. However, this time I drove it around to a place where I could park it and leave it for good, grab my two bags, and jump into a cab. The busy streets do not permit cars to park, however, so I drove away from the street and found an alley where several cars were already parked. As I drove up the end of the alley, I parked the car, took my bags, and ran into a small office to call for a cab.

I prayed so hard for a cab, and while I was praying, I found myself talking to a man behind the counter, upon which I discovered this was the National Car Rental office! Not only that, there were also several others waiting for a shuttle bus to take them to the same ship! The man said I could go with them. When I told him of my terrifying experience with the wrong addresses, he

My picture after safely boarding the SS Emerald Seas after a terrifying experience with wrong addresses.

called his home office immediately and reported the people who were giving customers old, outdated address information. Others came in to ride along on the same bus. We all rejoiced about how I got there on time to get on the bus and reach the *SS Emerald Seas.* (See my picture after this harrowing experience on this page.)

When I finally boarded the ship, Dr. and Mrs. Kennedy were there to shake my hand and direct me to a nice large cabin. Charles "Tremendous" Jones also greeted me with his famous hug (if you have not been hugged

Dr. and Mrs. D. James Kennedy pose with Clarence on the 1988 Coral Ridge Cruise.

by Charlie, you simply *have not been hugged!*). Words cannot reveal the great relief and joy and thanks to God for answering my prayers through His secret agents—holy angels that led me to drive up that strange alley and board that bus. I felt like my life was saved by God's supernatural power, and I will continue to thank and praise Him every day as long as I live. That is why I believe I am still going strong past 90. By the way, the cruise and the fellowship on the high seas are among the most memorable of my life.

The following 4 page brochure is reprinted in response to the many inquires as to ..."How Prayer Breakfast Groups Were Started!"

Baltimore Fellowship Foundation, Inc.

t/a The Baltimore Breakfast Group

How Prayer Breakfast Groups Were Started!

In the 1930's, during a time of intense political stress and corruption in the City of Seattle, Washington, W.H. St. Clair, Fred Ernst, Major J.F. Douglas and sixteen other civic leaders, led by Abraham Vereide, the founder/leader who developed the prayer breakfast movement, met at the Olympic Hotel and dedicated themselves to a three-fold spiritual program:

✟ *That each man would focus his attention on his own personal needs to put his life and business in order.*

✟ *That each man would turn to God in penitence and prayer to ask forgiveness, grace and guidance.*

✟ *That each man would study holy scripture to put its teachings to work in his own home, his business and his civic life.*

The requirement was to become a practicing New Testament Christian in every area of each man's life.

Over the years, as various men told other men how much this small group of believers meant to them, other prayer breakfast groups were begun through the State of Washington, until such outreaches extended from San Francisco eastward to the City of Chicago, then to Boston, Philadelphia and finally to the Nation's Capital in Washington, DC in the year 1941.

Soon afterward a band of businessmen, whose hearts God had touched, started a prayer breakfast which is known as **The Baltimore Breakfast Group**, who also sponsors the Baltimore Mayor's and Governor's Prayer Breakfasts.

Prayer Breakfast Groups were started in the United States Congress, the Senate and the House of Representatives, which proposed the simple idea that professional, business and government leaders – both men and women – could meet together on a weekly basis, early in the day, for Bible study, prayer and mutual encouragement and fellowship, to find "the better way" of life in honoring their Creator as God. This idea has spread to forty countries and in every continent on this globe.

On February 5, 1953, President Dwight D. Eisenhower inaugurated the first Presidential Prayer Breakfast in the main ballroom of the Mayflower Hotel, Washington, DC. Harry Hitchcock, Paul Hughes, Dr. John Evans, Clarence Hottel and many members of the United States Congress were in attendance. Conrad Hilton was the host. **Billy Graham** and **President Eisenhower** were the keynote speakers and **Jerome Hines,** with his marvelous voice, sang the great hymns of our faith and gave an inspiring testimony.

Since the year 1959, governors of over forty-five states have joined with the President to hold continuing Governors' Prayer Breakfasts in their own political jurisdictions. Many cities throughout the nation hold regular City government leadership prayer breakfasts in the same manner as we do in Baltimore.

Over the years we have been fortunate to obtain many outstanding guest speakers, such as Corrie ten Boom, Dr. J. Vernon McGee, Hal Lindsey, Jerry Falwell, Dr. Robert A. Cook, and Dr. Billy Graham in June 1981 with 4,000 in attendance at the Baltimore Convention Center. The Fifteenth Annual Mayor's Prayer Breakfast was held on May 10, 1985 with Charles Colson as guest speaker and two thousand attendees present. This is typical of what the average attendance has been each year in the past.

In November 1987 the **First Maryland Governor's Prayer Breakfast** was held at the Baltimore Convention Center with the ballroom filled. Dr. D. James Kennedy and the Honorable John Ashcroft (Governor of Missouri) were keynote speakers. On May 26, 1989 the Second Maryland Governor's Prayer Breakfast was held with Charles "Tremendous" Jones as the keynote speaker. The Third Maryland Governor's Prayer Breakfast was held on November 19, 1990 with broadcast and print journalist Cal Thomas as the keynote speaker. On December 16, 1994 the Fourth Maryland Governor's Prayer Breakfast was held with Dr. Richard C. Halverson, Chaplain of the United States Senate, as the keynote speaker.

The Baltimore Breakfast Group is affiliated with the National Fellowship Foundation which directs the Presidental Prayer Breakfast in our Nation's Capital every year, usually held the first Thursday in February.

We are a non-profit, non-denominational fellowship composed of concerned men and women who believe that the Bible is the infallible Word of God and that there is power in prayer to change things for the good of all citizens who place their faith and trust in Him.

The Baltimore Breakfast Group meets the last Friday of each month, 7:30 a.m. We are currently meeting at the Radisson Hotel at Cross Keys, Village of Cross Keys, 5100 Falls Road, Baltimore, MD 21210… just ten minutes from downtown Baltimore and Camden Yards!

You will enjoy and appreciate the encouragement in the faith at these friendly breakfast meetings...
ample, free parking.
Looking forward to seeing you...bring a friend!

For information please telephone
410-771-9400, 800-787-6000,
or fax **410-891-1542.**

Baltimore Fellowship Foundation, Inc.

Clarence W. Hottel, Sr., President
Dorothy L. Drinkwater, Secretary

STATE OF MARYLAND
OFFICE OF THE GOVERNOR

IN REPLY REFER TO

WILLIAM DONALD SCHAEFER
GOVERNOR

ANNAPOLIS OFFICE
STATE HOUSE
ANNAPOLIS, MARYLAND 21401
(301) 974-3901

BALTIMORE OFFICE
ROOM 1513
301 WEST PRESTON STREET
BALTIMORE, MARYLAND 21201
(301) 225-4800

WASHINGTON OFFICE
SUITE 315
444 NORTH CAPITOL STREET, N.W.
WASHINGTON, D.C. 20001
(202) 638-2215

TDD (301) 333-3098

December 1, 1987

Mr. Clarence W. Hottel
Chairman of the Board
Fidelity Engineering Corporation
10915 McCormick Road
Hunt Valley, Maryland 21031

Dear Mr Hottel

What a great event! I am writing to personally thank you for
organizing our First Annual Governor's Prayer Breakfast. It
was certainly a very moving and enlightening spiritual
experience for everyone who attended. I just wanted you to
know how pleased I was to take part in such a joyous and
thoroughly rewarding occasion.

I also appreciated the devoted efforts of Dorothy Drinkwater,
Reverend Les Metcalf and Herb Fivehouse. Together, you made
quite a team! Long ago, I learned the tremendous value of the
prayer breakfast. I learned the importance of faith and
friendship, and also about spiritual renewal. I am deeply
appreciative of your commitment and your caring.

Please be assured that my warmest wishes shall remain with all
of you throughout the Holidays and into next year!

Sincerely,

Governor

The Fine Art of Leadership

If you want to rule, learn to serve;
if you want to lead, learn to follow;
if you want to succeed,
learn to make others succeed.
—Woodrow Kroll

In their marvelous book on leadership, *Everyone's a Coach,* retired football coach Don Shula and management consultant and author Ken Blanchard team up to provide some of the finest insights in print today on what it means to be a true success in life—to follow not where the path may lead, but instead where there is *no* road and to leave a trail for others to follow. For almost 200 pages, they write about becoming a success, how to live with that success, and how to go head-to-head with the opposition, difficulty, and despair that will surely come our way. It's powerful stuff.

While virtually all the stories in the book are motivational, none is more poignant than when Blanchard writes about one of his consultant friends, Barbara Glanz, who was conducting a customer service session for a large retail grocery company in the Midwest. As Barbara spoke to a large crowd of front-line service people—cashiers, baggers, stockers, butchers, bakers, and others—she told the assembled audience they all needed to figure out a way to do whatever possible to put their own signature on their job. To help them understand what she meant, she asked the group just one question: *What could you do that is uniquely you?* Three weeks after her talk, Barbara received a telephone call from a 19-year-old bagger named Johnny, who has Down's syndrome. Here is the rest of this amazing story, as it appears in the book:

> *"The night after I heard you speak to us, my parents and I talked about what I could do special for my customers. I've collected good quotations over the years, and we decided I would give them to the people I served at the store." He went on to tell her that he typed his list of quotes on the family computer, made 150 copies of each, and then cut them out and folded them. The next day, he chose one of his quotes, and when he finished bagging a customer's groceries, he would say, "I'm putting my quote for the day in your bag. I hope it makes your day."*

When Johnny tried to usher some of the people into other lines, no one would leave. "They all wanted to get my quote for the day," said Johnny.

> *The day Johnny called Barbara, the store manager was making his rounds. When he got to the front of the store, he noticed that all the customers were in Johnny's aisle. When Johnny tried to usher some of the people into other lines, no one would leave. "They all wanted to get my quote for the day," said Johnny.*

Barbara followed up the story by calling the store manager. The manager said, "One of the customers told me, 'I used to shop here once a week; now I stop by here every day.' Since the kid's success, everybody on my staff tries to do special things for customers! For example, the butcher likes Snoopy, and now when people pick up their orders, the packages are sealed with Snoopy stickers. When flowers are damaged, the folks in a flower shop are cutting the broken stems off and making corsages for our customers shopping in our store. Everybody who works here has caught the spirit that Johnny started!" Don Shula & Ken Blanchard, *Everyone's a Coach* (New York: Harper Business, 1995), p.33.

What a story . . . and one that provides irrefutable proof that you and I do not have to enjoy a certain IQ, be of any particular race, be highly educated, or even have a high level of training in leadership skills to catch a vision for helping others and put that vision into practice. Young Johnny had Down's syndrome, but he refused to allow his disability to prevent him from making a difference in the lives of his customers. From that simple list of 150 quotes came the

> *I can say we have been able to be successful as leaders in our field of work only because of the grace of God.*

kind of inspiration that changed the attitude and spirit of an entire store and touched the hearts of hundreds of customers.

What an incredible example of servant leadership. When someone catches a vision—and is able to communicate the power of that vision to others—that person is a leader. It is my hope that as people look at the service record of Fidelity Engineering Corporation over the past five decades, they will see that same kind of leadership in the hearts and brains of our employees. If that is the legacy of our company, then my work at Fidelity Engineering will have been a resounding success.

Anatomy of a Successful Leader

As I look back over the many years of heating and air conditioning service to our customers, I can say we have been able to be successful as leaders in our field of work only because of the grace of God. Further, when people ask me to define the "anatomy" of a leader, my first answer is always that the best leadership is usually acquired innocently: you simply do good work, keep on doing it, share your goals and dreams with others, and never quit. Often, the greatest leaders are not aware of the depth of their contributions at the time they are making their impact. Perhaps that is because true leadership is divinely instituted, where the leader is simply the channel through whom God works to do His bidding. Over the years, I never recall telling anyone, "Look here now, I'm the boss. It's my way or the highway." Such puffery was never necessary—and I

> **Over the years, I never recall telling anyone, "Look here now, I'm the boss. It's my way or the highway."**

doubt that it would have been very productive. If there is a secret to effective leadership, however, it will probably be found among the following ideas, shared by some of the most successful men and women in the world of business. See if you agree:

• **Worry about the little things and the larger issues will take care of themselves.**

• **Spend the extra time to maintain your equipment. People do not have to brush all their teeth either—only the ones they want to keep.**

• **The race is not always won by the fastest runner but sometimes by those who just keep running. (That's how we felt during the Great Depression.)**

• **We do not stop working because we are old; we grow old because we stop working.**

• **Never hold a $1,000 meeting to solve a $100 problem.**

• **Learn from the mistakes of others. None of us will live long enough to make them all ourselves.**

• **And this great quote from the famed inventor Thomas Edison: If we did all the things we are capable of doing, we would literally astound ourselves.**

However, as good and profound as these quotes may be, they all pale in comparison to the powerful success principle of all, found in Psalm 1. This short passage of Scripture has been my guide through life. It has lifted me when I have needed God's special touch in my personal and professional life, and it continues to sustain me today. It can do the same for you. As you read this profound chapter, focus on the "heart" of the passage, which gives you God's formula for prosperity and success:

Blessed is the man
    who does not walk in the counsel of the wicked
or stand in the way of sinners
    or sit in the seat of mockers.
But his delight is in the law of the LORD,
    and on his law he meditates day and night.
He is like a tree planted by streams of water,
    which yields its fruit in season
and whose leaf does not wither.
    Whatever he does prospers.

Not so the wicked!
    They are like chaff
    that the wind blows away.
Therefore the wicked will not stand in the judgment,
    nor sinners in the assembly of the righteous.
For the LORD *watches over the way of the righteous,*
    but the way of the wicked will perish.

                                      (NIV)

Prosperity comes to those who delight in the Law of God. Success in leadership comes to the men and women who continually *meditate* (the Hebrew word for a cow chewing her cud) on God's good, friendly, life-sustaining laws. Like the tree that receives its nourishment from fresh streams of living water, the person who taps into the power of the living God enjoys a life of success. All this, combined with a passion for people, a commitment to service, and a promise to be faithful in all things, are the ingredients of a successful leader.

However, there is another element that unleashes the greatest energy of all: *the power of prayer.* Several years ago, my buddy Charlie "Tremendous" Jones asked me to recommend one of my favorite books to his readers, one that had made the greatest impact on my life. I chose *George Muller, Man of Faith and Miracles,* because it had always been my life's desire to live by the principles that had guided this great servant of God. The words I wrote for Charlie those many years ago are the same words I would use if he asked me to write them today:

Charles "Tremendous" Jones has spoken at the Maryland Governor's Prayer Breakfast and the regular Baltimore Breakfast Group meetings.

Mr. Muller is one of the greatest prayer warriors of the past century, and his biography has meant much to me for many years, particularly in the way he sought to know the will of God. The following six points have been his guide, which I try to follow:

1. I seek at the beginning to get my heart into such a state that it has no will of its own in regard to a given matter.

2. Having done this, I do not leave the result to feeling or simple impressions. If so, I make myself liable to great delusions.

3. I seek the will of the Spirit of God through or in connection with the Word of God. The Spirit and the Word must be combined.

*4. Next, I take into account providential circum-
stances. These plainly indicate God's will in connection with His Word and Spirit.*

5. I ask God in prayer to reveal His will to me aright.

*6. Thus through prayer to God, the study of the Word,
and reflection, I come to a deliberate judgment...*

Leaders Are People of Purpose

Harvey and I always tried to live our lives with
great purpose. We worked diligently to become successful businessmen; however, we also determined
to be a credit to our father and mother, who worked
hard to grow each church to which the Mennonite
Conference assigned them for more than 50 years.
We never forgot our roots,
the quality of the training
we received, or the love so
freely given to us by our
parents. When Harvey and I
began our fledgling radio
business as teenagers, we
had no idea where our
paths might lead us, but we
always knew our lives had
significance and purpose,
and we lived with the daily
awareness that God would
keep on doing good things
in our lives—a constant
thought that not only took

> ...that God would keep
> on doing good things
> in our lives...not only
> took us through the
> Depression, but helped
> us actually thrive
> during that terrible time
> in American history.

us through the Depression, but helped us actually
thrive during that terrible time in American history.

Charles E. Jones, editor, *The People You Meet and the Books You Read* (Harrisburg, Pa.: Executive Books, 1986), p. 123.

Because we took our dad's counsel on how to start our business enterprises, which was to found and manage separate companies in different locations so we would not be competitors, Harvey and I were able to assume industry leadership roles in the Washington and Baltimore areas. Before long, Harvey also became treasurer of Fourth Presbyterian Church in Bethesda, Maryland, where he worked closely with his beloved pastor, Dr. Richard C. Halverson, who later became chaplain of the

Three Hottel brothers (left to right: Harvey, Winfred and Clarence) at Harvey's Piper Twin Engine plane. For many years Harvey was his pastor's personal small plane pilot. Date 1969.

United States Senate. Harvey was a trusted friend and confidant of Dr. Halverson for many years, and was even his personal small-plane pilot, taking his pastor to various speaking engagements across the nation, saving him hundreds of hours in valuable time and thousands of dollars in expenses. Harvey would always consider this one of his most important ministries, and he loved it.

Just a few miles away, in the city of Baltimore, my family and I attended the Park Heights Presbyterian Church, where Dr. T. Roland Philips was pastor. Through the years I was involved in a number of church positions. Yes, Harvey and I were busy engineering, making sales calls, learning the new technology, and making money, but we never forgot the magnitude of our first love—our

Savior and Lord Jesus Christ. He was always pre-eminent in our lives.

Now, as I look back over nine decades of life, I have to say that for all the crazy things we did as twin brothers over the years—more mistakes and miscues than I care to mention—the Lord never once took His gentle hand off our shoulders. I leave it to others to determine whether we have been faithful servants. I simply trust that the jury will give both Harvey and me the benefit of the doubt.

> *Trust God implicitly.*
> *If you are united with Him,*
> *nothing can harm you.*

A Leader Is Secure

I don't think a great deal about security, and never have. However, when pressed to define it, I have no choice but to fall back on the promise of God clearly articulated in John 3:16: "For God so loved the world that he gave his one and only Son, that whoever believes in him shall not perish but have eternal life" (NIV). Security is feeling safe and protected no matter how great the storm. As a Christian leader, I have seldom felt it necessary to rely on material things to feel secure. Whenever I have done so, it has been disaster. Instead, I have always tried to take comfort in the Lord's promise that He would never leave me or forsake me. Hebrews 13:5–6 in the Contemporary English Version reads, "The Lord helps me! Why should I be afraid of what people can do to me?" A poet follows up this thought by saying,

> *He gives me joy in place of sorrow,*
> *He gives me love that casts out fear,*
> *He gives me sunshine for my shadows*
> *And beauty for ashes here.*

To this I would add, *trust God implicitly. If you are united with Him, nothing can harm you.* Over the years, I have discovered the Lord is always ready to help us in times of distress. However, we have a responsibility to work and excel at an honest trade if we are to see our dreams come true. Occasionally I hear people say, "It seems that the harder I work, the luckier I get." There is truth in that statement. Hard work pays off. There is no way around it. The "when I win the lottery" mentality will send a person to the poorhouse. Success in leadership demands work. Did you know that the word *easy* appears only once in the New Testament, and then only in connection with the word yoke—which implies work! Second Thessalonians 3:10 also makes it clear: "We also gave you the rule that if

Balance is the key to stress management

you don't work, you don't eat" (CEV). For this reason, when your fragile boat of finance, relationships, or physical health begins to take on water, you must do two things: pray to God and row for shore. It's an unbeatable combination.

A Leader Manages Stress

There is no way out of stress, unless it is death itself. Leaders, especially, must learn to manage this demon, which can rear its head at any provocation and render the best-laid plans ineffective. Balance is the key to stress management: balance between office and family; balance between work and play; balance between a healthy body and a healthy mind. We as leaders—and we are all leaders in one way or another, as parents, business executives, employees, coaches, ministers, small-business owners, Scout leaders, Sunday School teachers, etc.— understand stress management best when we recognize the truth of Scripture, which says, "Your own body does not belong to you. For God has bought you with a great price. So use

> **I have always tried to rely on God's promises and live in His strength...**

every part of your body to give glory back to God, because he owns it" (1 Corinthians 6:19–20, *The Living Bible*).

Perhaps I have been wired differently from many, but stress has not been a major issue in my life. Problems, yes. Mountains of challenges? No question about it. However, I have always tried to rely on God's promises and live in His strength, trusting Him for all outcomes in all situations. I remember how my faith was severely put to the test the day I suffered the loss of Dottie, my dear wife and partner. It was a terrible blow. I had lost my best friend. However, instead of succumbing to the reality of her death with shock, bewilderment, anger, and anxiety, I knew I would be better served if I used that time of sadness to rededicate my life, my family, and my company, Fidelity Engineering Corporation, to the Lord. With God's help, I feel I did that, not that it was easy.

Dottie (at top) with grandaughters (left to right) Beth, Nancy, Susan, son Bill and his wife Sally. Date 1979. My faith was severely put to the test the day that I suffered the loss of Dottie, my dear wife and partner.

Hard Work: A Leader's Legacy

The leader who has lived a full life, who has been active, aggressive, and living on the edge of accomplishment, will undoubtedly have a full "in tray" when he or she dies. It is simply the nature of business. There is always one more deal to close, one more contract to sign, one more heating and air conditioning unit to install, one more sales call to make, and one more customer to serve. All my life I have wished there were more hours in the day. There has always been so much to do and never enough hours to do it.

It must be the same with any good employee. Dependable workers do not leave at five o'clock (having watched the clock closely since 4:30 to make sure the big and little hands are still moving!), neglecting something that will disappoint a customer or hinder another employee from doing his or her job in the morn-

> ## *Dependable workers do not leave at five o'clock...*

ing. An employee who leaves things incomplete lowers his or her earning power, and is like so many fine grains of sand that grate on bearings, instead of being a team player who lubricates the machinery to help his fellow workers do their work better and more efficiently, thus increasing the earning power of everyone involved in the project. Some employees accept their regular, dependable paycheck with the idea that the world owes them a living—even though they know they have been less than honest and dependable in their work. Such a person must ask himself, *"What really is* my earning power?" If this individual had struggled through the Great Depression, the idea of a "free lunch" would never see the light of day. The following Scripture verses, taken from *The Living Bible,* have a great deal to say about the rewards promised to the one who does good, hard, honest work—and they are applicable to anyone in the work place:

Hard work means prosperity; only a fool idles away his time (Proverbs 12:11).

Work brings profit; talk brings poverty! (Proverbs 14:23).

Do you know a hard-working man? He shall be successful and stand before kings! (Proverbs 22:29).

Whatever you do, do well, for in death, where you are going, there is no working or planning, or knowing, or understanding (Ecclesiastes 9:10).

This should be your ambition: to live a quiet life, minding your own business and doing your own work, just as we told you before. As a result, people who are not Christians will trust and respect you, and you will not need to depend on others for enough money to pay your bills (1 Thessalonians 4:11–12).

Building Blocks of a Leader

There has never been anything made that some man cannot make a little poorer and sell a little cheaper. The sweetness of low price never equals the bitterness of low quality! Fidelity Engineering Corporation has always lived by this business standard. Over the years, we have also learned that it pays to listen carefully to what a customer wants and needs— after which it is our task to survey the job site, develop a full understanding of all the conditions and requirements—including utilities—prepare a detailed estimate sheet, and finally come to a true cost, from which we arrive at a proper and fair selling price. From that point on, it takes a well-trained, experienced technician to prove to the buyer that we are the company best suited to do the job. But it all begins with an attentive ear.

Another building block that helped Fidelity Engineering Corporation become a major industry leader over the years is that customers knew our company's employees were under the management and ownership of Christian-principled stockholders who pledged their allegiance to the Ten Commandments. Even today, in an increasingly secularized world, we give free Bibles to every employee. Our original commitment has always been to the principles of Psalm 1, where God promises, "Whatever he does prospers." I sincerely hope that everyone who reads this book will go back to page 190 in this chapter and read Psalm 1 repeatedly. These verses have been the foundation of our company, and I am confident that God has granted us leadership success because we have relied on His strength and the wisdom of this psalm.

> **Maintain your enthusiasm— it is 90 percent of your success.**

Although I officially retired in March 1990, I'm probably busier now than ever. I simply cannot retire if I am forced to agree with the definition provided by Webster: "to withdraw from action . . . to withdraw esp. for privacy . . . to withdraw from one's position or occupation: conclude one's working or professional career." That kind of life sounds like no life to me. Here's why. I still feel a great sense of purpose for my life. I hope you feel the same way, regardless of your age or position. If you have developed worthy goals and objectives, there is a good chance that you, too, will never retire. In your position of leadership, continue to surround yourself with dependable people who agree with the principles you have set forth and who are willing to move ahead with you. Maintain your enthusiasm—it is 90 percent of your success. When followers have confidence in their leader, the sky is the limit.

Although I am no longer responsible for day-to-day operations, I maintain an office at the company and at home and continue to do what I can to encourage our employees to be at their best. I have willingly taken "hands off" the company and have moved myself "upstairs" as founder/chairman emeritus. Even so, my passion for Fidelity Engineering Corporation's growth in the new millennium

Clarence Hottel in his Company office. His new freedom gives him even more time for personal ministry, as he devotes much of his time and resources to the Baltimore Prayer Breakfast Group and other Christian causes.

continues unabated. My new freedom, however, gives me even more time for personal ministry, as I devote much of my time and resources to the Baltimore Prayer Breakfast Group and other Christian causes.

In 1999, when I celebrated my 91st birthday at a party with the staff at The King's College in the Empire State Building in New York City, I was again reminded of my long relationship with its founder, Percy Crawford, and the college itself, a friendship that has been dear to my heart for many years—actually, since I was 16 years old. However, I would not be honest if I said this was not a time for reflection on my personal and business life. I have the luxury of looking back, seeing the large canvas on which I have painted the pictures of my life, of remembering the lives I have touched—and those lives who have touched me so profoundly.

> *I will be grateful to her as wife and mother for every day that God gives me breath.*

From the very beginning, my wife, Dottie, Co-Founder of Fidelity Engineering Corporation, was responsible for office management. What would I have done without her business and people skills in those early days of our young, upstart company? I will be grateful to her as wife and mother for every day that God gives me breath. My sons Bill and Jim were never asked to join the company; however, in their teen years, they would automatically put on their overalls, equip themselves with the latest tool kits

Today, Bill(center) is president/CEO of Fidelity Engineering Corporation, and his daughters, Elizabeth (seated) and Susan (not shown), both play pivotal roles in the life of our growing organization.

and instruments (each driving his own fully equipped truck), and go out on Fidelity Engineering jobs after school. Eventually, they both grew up to become owners and leaders in the company under the watchful eyes of their mother and father. Today, Bill is president/CEO of Fidelity Engineering Corporation, and his daughters, Elizabeth and Susan, both play pivotal roles in the life of our growing organization. Elizabeth graduated from Bucknell University and today is a professional engineer and vice president of the Engineering Division of Fidelity Engineering Corporation. Susan graduated from Western Maryland College and works with her sister in the same department. Jim is presently working for a consulting team, which surveys large buildings that face the challenges of modernizing their HVAC systems.

Leadership Is the Key

With all its rich heritage of success, Fidelity Engineering Corporation continues to be a leading mechanical engineering firm with diversified interests and capabilities, such as HVAC service, generators, controls, and construction. Construction department projects include IHS Headquarters (Integrated Health Services), MBC Realty (Mercantile Bank), Super Fresh at Timonium Fairgrounds Plaza, Timonium I and II office buildings, Columbia Corporate Park, Hecht's Department Store in Fair Oaks, Virginia, and the new Lord & Taylor store at Owings Mills Mall, to name only a few. As I review our current contracts, however, I cannot help but think back to what Victor Frenkil said to me in the early days of our company: "You do the right thing for Mr. Graham, and your company will have it made in Baltimore." Well, I don't know if we have it made or not, but I can say with gratitude to the people of Baltimore and the surrounding area that it continues to be a pleasure to serve them with their heating and air conditioning needs—a commitment that Fidelity Engineering Corporation will continue long after the Lord takes me to heaven.

Over the years, I have kept careful records of our company's achievements, and it amazes me to see how far we have come technologically since the 1940s and 1950s, when air conditioning was relatively new. When we started Fidelity Engineering Corporation, we had only three employees (two refrigeration technicians and a secretary) and

Dorothy. Because Dorothy was doing so much of the administrative work, it was soon necessary to hire a full-time housekeeper, Nellie Summers, to relieve my wife of the many household duties that otherwise would not have been attended to. What would we have done without dear Nellie!

Today, we have more than 150 fully equipped vans, trucks, trailers, and cars, with 312 employees.

We started with one pickup and one service truck; today, we have more than 150 fully equipped vans, trucks, trailers, and cars. Half a century of hiring all kinds of employees also helped me learn how to avoid those individuals who detested hard work, wasted time, and were otherwise unproductive—but who still wanted the money and the accompanying awards. After a while, I could see them coming a mile away, and few, if any, became part of the Fidelity Engineering team.

Today, Fidelity Engineering Corporation has seven divisions, each with its own leader or manager who is required to provide an account of the division at a weekly meeting with top management. A leader, then, in each division is appointed manager because he or she has the capacity to direct his colleagues with a full knowledge of our business and an equal dose of enthusiasm. Here are the four keys to the success of these leaders at Fidelity. He or she...

1. is willing to be a servant, ready to help anyone on the team to succeed. The best servant often automatically becomes the appointed leader.

2. is willing to spend the extra time and energy to meet an unexpected, urgent customer need, refusing to leave the job site until the client's system is in full operation.

3. is willing to study to develop the skills to do our business; to follow the ASHRAE and manufacturers' manuals; to be alert mentally and intellectually. Free "five minutes a day" New Testaments are available at the front desk for spiritual reflection—something as important as the mandatory physical checkup.

> Everyone has the capacity to lead, regardless of position or salary.

4. is willing and prepared to obey all laws, maintain a careful driving record, and is careful not to offend others on the road.

Whether consistent, unfailing leadership is displayed by a Fidelity Engineering Corporation truck driver, engineer, custodian, secretary, sheet metal cutter, foreman, or the president/CEO himself, it is invariably the one quality that always separates the best from the good. Everyone has the capacity to lead, regardless of position or salary. Everyone is vital to the company's success. No one is more important or has greater value than another. I think you will agree with me as I close this chapter with the insightful words of Dr. Richard C. Halverson, taken from *Perspective,* September 9, 1996.

Harvey Hottel (right) celebrates his company's 50th anniversay with Dr. and Mrs. Richard C. Halverson (center) and Clarence Hottel (left).

Dear Friend,

How important are you?

Anytime you begin to feel you aren't worth very much, consider this:

You are a "key" person.

Xvxn though my typxwritxr is an old modxl, it works vxry wxll

xxcxpt for onx kxy.

You would think that with all thx othxr kxys functioning propxrly onx kxy not working would hardly bx noticxd, but just onx kxy out of whack sxxms to ruin thx wholx xffort.

You may say to yourself, 'Wxll, I'm only onx pxrson, no onx will xvxn noticx if I don't quitx do my bxst.'

But it doxs makx a diffxrxncx bxcausx to bx xffxctivx, an organization nxxds activx participation by xvxry onx to thx bxst of his or hxr ability.

207

So thx nxxt timx you think you arx not important, rxmxmbxr my old typxwritxr.

You are a kxy person!

"'Are not two sparrows sold for a penny? Yet not one of them will fall to the ground apart from the will of your Father. And even the very hairs of your head are all numbered. So don't be afraid; you are worth more than many sparrows'" (Matthew 10:29–31, NIV). [3]

---

[3] Richard C. Halverson, *Perspective* Vol. 43, No. 24 (Sep. 9, 1996).

40th ANNIVERSARY MESSAGE from Clarence W. Hottel, Sr.

On Knowing Fidelity Better

by Clarence W. Hottel, Sr.

From A Quick View Backward To A Forward View Ahead

Having reached forty years of continuous business success, may we allow ourselves to take a look backward!

The many good companies we serve and deal with, certainly our 125 employees, also vendors and subcontractors, are forward thinking people and it is a little out of character for us to look backward. However, this being our 40th year in 1985, as FIDELITY celebrates, it seems appropriate to reflect upon just a few of the many signposts we have passed and a little upon our origin.

Where We Came From

It really started when my Dad (a Mennonite minister) was stationed in Philadelphia to pastor a church where my twin brother, Harvey, and I learned from one of the church parishioners, who worked for the research department of the telephone company, how to build radios. We sold as well as serviced hundreds of them—from crystal sets to superheterodynes.

Unexcelled Service Is The Key

We learned very early in our teen years that customers believe in you implicitly in proportion to the way you know your business and give them good, honest, prompt service and make their installation work at peak efficiency.

Training And Working On The Job Generates The Thrill

While high school students in Bethlehem, Pennsylvania, where our family was stationed to a new large church, we continued in the radio business and then added appliances, commercial refrigeration and air conditioning. The business grew; the industry was new, and we took advantage of all the manufacturers' technical data and training schools. There were no schools or colleges at that time teaching a course on air conditioning application/service. We learned by studying and doing it in the field, working night and day with our own hands, as we sold and did each installation, which became the most thrilling desire of our lives.

209

The Art Of Handling Air Like A Fluid

I distinctly recall a large sign high above the podium in front of the classroom in the Syracuse plant where Dr. Willis Carrier himself (the chief, and inventor of air conditioning) taught us the science of thermodynamics in applying mechanical refrigeration and explained how to use the psychrometric chart he invented. The sign read, CARRIER KNOWS THE ART OF HANDLING AIR. This indelibly impressed me. I have never forgotten it; also, how Dr. Carrier personally took us through the plant. The Frigidaire Division of General Motors also provided technical training courses from which my brother and I were graduated.

Study, With Practical Experience And Good Business Management Essential

Even today not too many people who try to design and attempt to apply air conditioning, heating and humidity control equipment fully know and understand the art of properly installing and servicing systems. Handling air like a fluid is truly a highly specialized art. Temperature, humidity controls, number of air changes per hour, distribution, noise level, etc., and complying with the ASHRAE comfort zone chart conditions, which we guarantee, requires experienced design, installation and service technicians to install an efficient system. FIDELITY has the factory-trained people able to accomplish this!

Move To Baltimore

Through the Carrier Company's persuasion, as they observed "Hottel installations" in Pennsylvania, my wife, Dorothy, and I moved to Baltimore where the potential was much greater and I worked for Carrier until the Second World War was over, finally in charge of the Baltimore distributor branch.

In 1945, on our dining room table, we started FIDELITY with several former Carrier distributor employees. Harvey did the same in his area of Washington, D.C.

Keeping up with the schooling available, mainly through the Carrier Company, Frigidaire and other manufacturers; as an active member and diligent student of the American Society of Heating, Refrigerating and Air Conditioning Engineers, Inc. data books (considered the bibles of the industry); later becoming President of the Baltimore Washington Chapter, provided our Company with the know-how and advancement to become a leader in its field as the industry demand grew. The Carrier Company also taught good business management principles which are still appreciated, admired and used to this day!

210

Hottel Sons Join Company

Growth took a great step forward as my sons, Bill and Jim, grew up in the Company. Both Bill (President) and Jim (Executive Vice-President) promptly acquired the same thrill of seeing their design and application of equipment function in the field. Endeavoring to be diligent and Christian-principled business men, as taught by my parents, has brought about customer confidence and sales of thousands of installations with many of the largest companies in the country. We have become a multi-million dollar Company thanks to Bill and Jim's outstanding ability. They are now acknowledged by our customers and suppliers, even our competitors, as the most competent ASHRAE design and build men in this entire area.

The growth of our multi-faceted business created the need for a larger plant and facilities. We have two large buildings in the beautiful Hunt Valley Industrial Park providing space for our offices, Kohler generators, John Deere and White engines, Parts Department, Construction Department with architectural, piping and sheet metal divisions, and Energy Management Department. We also have a branch in York, Pennsylvania.

Fidelity Has Developed The Finest Computer Room Installation Technique Available Today

Going forward in great strides, my sons have, with good key people, aggressively gone after the computer room business — *designing a complete package for the entire room, including back-up generators, Halon fire suppression systems, raised floors with specially designed air conditioning units with filtering and humidity control* — backed up by our economical Maintenance Contracts and unexcelled emergency service, 24 hours a day!

With the development of the Data Processing industry over the last twenty years, our firm has specialized in the design and installation of computer rooms, made ready on a "turn key" basis including every item necessary to prepare the room tailored to the exacting environmental requirements for today's sophisticated equipment. Within this discipline we have prepared hundreds of rooms for major computer users from coast to coast. Our attention to computer facilities has made our Company a leader with firms planning to build and/or expand their Data Processing operations.

Excellent Employee Relationships And Valued Customers Have Made our 40 Years of Growth Possible

Congratulations to all of our faithful employees who study in our training schools to keep up with all the latest techniques and developments! This

211

helps us to turn many problems into solutions for our customers and our dreams into actual realities. We also want to extend our sincere appreciation to our many valued customers with whom we enjoy close productive and cordial daily relationships.

Having reviewed some of the past and how we have succeeded, now we want to turn our attention to the future and concentrate on the coming 50th Anniversary with the same forward thinking and planning that brought us to where we are today!

I have always looked forward to my sons continuing to take the lead and operate FIDELITY with honest, diligent, hard-working employees.

God has honored our faithfulness over the years. The conditions of prosperity for anyone are found in Psalm 1 and Proverbs 22:29.

Thus we cannot fail!

CHAPTER 10

The Road Ahead

If you make the Most High your dwelling—
even the Lord, who is my refuge—then no harm
will befall you, no disaster will come near your tent.
For he will command his angels concerning you
to guard you in all your ways.
—Psalm 91:9–11 (NIV)

Actor Jimmy Stewart once spoke of an incident that occurred just before his bomber squadron was preparing to leave for a European mission during World War II. As the last few minutes ticked away before leaving home, Jimmy felt that his father wanted to say something. But his dad was choked up, and nothing would come out of his mouth. Finally, saying nothing, his father embraced him and left the room. Only later did Jimmy discover that his dad had slipped a letter into his flight jacket, which said, "Soon you will be on your way to the worst of dangers. Let us both count on the promise contained in the enclosed psalm . . . I love you more than I can tell you" (paraphrased). Jimmy then read these words: "God will put His angels in charge of you to protect you wherever you go."

As I reflect on that moment between father and son, I find myself praising God that the same Heavenly Father who protected Jimmy Stewart during that terrible war is the same God who also has protected me for more than 91 years. He has been—and continues to be—a God of love, mercy, compassion, and protection. Still, I find it amazing how He chose to take a preacher's son who had tinkered with radios and sold home appliances and gave him the technical skills and organizational ability to begin Fidelity Engineering Cor-

> **Life is about relationships, and the ones that endure the test of time are the ones most satisfying.**

poration, an organization that continues to be a national leader in the heating and air conditioning field today. I, too, have been blessed with the same great truth of the Bible that promises, "God will put His angels in charge of you to protect you, your sons Bill and Jim, your daughter, Anne, their families, and all the employees, wherever they go."

Developing Relationships for a Lifetime

If we look back on our lives and discover we have only made money, driven fancy cars, owned a home in the suburbs, and spent the majority of our time pouring over the latest stock market quotes with our two best friends, Dow and Jones—and now their increasingly prosperous cousin, NASDAQ—I suggest we may have missed the boat. Life is about relationships, and the ones that endure the test of time are the ones most satisfying. It may be a grandchild's laughter, a spouse's humor and spontaneity, a friend's infectious warmth, or the thoughtfulness of a salesclerk at a local store. None of these have anything to do with material wealth, but they have everything in the world to do with happiness, joy, and contentment.

Just today I received the following note written by an 83-year-old woman to her friend. I think she puts life into a healthy, joyous perspective:

I'm reading more and dusting less. I'm sitting in the yard and admiring the view without fussing about the weeds in the garden. I'm spending more time with my family and friends and less time working. Whenever possible, life should be a pattern of experiences to savor, not to endure. I'm trying to recognize these moments now and cherish them. I'm not "saving" anything; I use my good china and crystal every time I eat. I wear my good blazer to the market. My theory is if I look prosperous, I can shell out $28.49 for one small bag of groceries.

And every morning when I open my eyes, I tell myself that it is special.

I'm not saving my good perfume for special parties, but wearing it for clerks in the hardware store and tellers at the bank. "Someday" and "one of these days" are losing their grip on my vocabulary. If it is worth seeing or hearing or doing, I want to see and hear and do it now!

I'm not sure what others would've done had they known that they wouldn't be here for the tomorrow

*that we take for granted. I think they would have
called family members and a few acquaintances.
They might have called a few former friends to apolo-
gize and mend fences for past squabbles. I think they
would have gone out for a Chinese dinner, or for
whatever their favorite food was. I'm guessing that
I'll never know.*

*It's those little things left undone that would make
me angry if I knew my hours were limited. Angry
because I hadn't written certain letters that I intended
to write one of these days. Angry and sorry that I did-
n't tell special people often enough how much I truly
love them. I'm trying very hard not to put off, hold
back, or save anything that would add laughter and
luster to my life. And every morning when I open my
eyes, I tell myself that it is special. Every day, every
minute, every breath truly is a gift from God.*

Maintaining a Positive Attitude

From the large living room window in our family
home in the Pocono mountains, I enjoy a ringside
seat to some of God's most beautiful creations—
birds, deer, raccoons, squirrels, even bears. I could
sit there all day watching these creatures of all
sizes, shapes, and color scurrying about or, in the
case of the bears, lumbering about. One day, an
interesting sight particularly impressed me. A fat
red robin was busily flitting about in a pouring
rain, stopping only momentarily to warble his
beautiful, trilling song. Unlike so many of the other birds on this rainy day, this feathered creature
was not seeking shelter from the downpour, but
was delighting himself in the shower that was
falling from heaven. Instinctively, the robin knew
the rain was making much valuable food available,

Our family home in the Pocono mountains...a ringside seat to some of God's most beautiful creations.

for the worms he sought would soon be near the surface and more plentiful in the dampened sod.

As I watched in delight, I thought of the torrents of trials and testing that have flooded my life over the past nine decades: the engineering deals that were not struck, the pain of the Great Depression, the deaths of my son and dear wife, the challenges of raising children. Or, were these really trials at all? How many times, I wonder, have I seen only the falling rain and not the great benefits that would soon come to me after a few moments of sadness, pain, and inconvenience.

I remember the story of Alexander Whyte, the famous Scottish preacher, who invariably began his public prayers with an expression of gratitude. One cold and rainy day when his people wondered how he could be grateful for the weather, he began by saying, "We thank Thee, O Lord, that it is not always like this." The good pastor realized that an appreciative heart brightens a dreary day and shortens the longest night. I ask myself, and I ask you my dear reader, as we approach the road ahead, is this attitude of positive expectation a key ingredient in our lives?

Karl Menninger tells a story about President Thomas Jefferson. One day the president "was traveling on horseback through the countryside with a group of companions. They came to a river and found that the bridge had been washed away by a recent rain. The only way across was to have their horses swim through the treacherous currents. Each rider took his life in his hands as they crossed. There was a good chance that some of them would not survive.

> **...people will remember us most for our small acts of kindness that invariably went unnoticed by the masses.**

"A man who was traveling on foot (who was not part of the group) was watching from a distance. Having seen several riders brave the currents, he walked up to the president and asked if he could ride across with him. Jefferson quickly agreed, and they took off across the water.

"When they arrived safely on the other side, the man slid off the saddle and onto the ground. One of the men from the president's group asked him, 'Tell me, why did you select the president to ride with?'

"Surprised, the man admitted that he hadn't known it was the president of the United States who had helped him across. 'All I know,' he said, 'is that on some of your faces was written the answer no, and on some of them was the answer yes. His was a yes face.'" [1]

Refining the Art of Appreciation

We all need love, affirmation, reinforcement, and appreciation. In all probability, you and I will be remembered not for our financial and material accomplishments. Rather, I think, people will remember us most for our small acts of kindness that invariably went unnoticed by the masses. Such small gestures have a powerful cumulative effect, whether it is walking through the offices and onto the factory floor of Fidelity Engineering Corporation to compliment our men and women on their good work, to be an encouragement to those who feel weak and inexperienced, to strengthen the bonds of the employer/employee relationship, or to help a frightened

God governs in the affairs of men.

child who feels sad and alone. Appreciation positively affects a person's self-image, brings strength to a family, and reminds our friends and associates that life would just not be the same without them. And let me put in a request that our loving voices

---

[1]Frank Martin, *War in the Pews* (Downers Grove, Ill.: InterVarsity Press, 1995), pp. 138–139.

speak these words of kindness, and not the greeting-card manufacturer. When we show genuine appreciation for our friends and associates, we also put ourselves in a brighter mood as we become aware of how blessed we really are.

Righteousness Exalts a Nation

Benjamin Franklin declared when framing the Constitution, "I have lived, sir, a long time; and the longer I live the more convincing proofs I see of this truth, that God governs in the affairs of men. If a sparrow cannot fall to the ground without His notice, is it probable that an empire can rise without His aid? We have been assured, sir, in the Sacred Writings, that 'except the Lord build the house, they labor in vain that build it.' I firmly believe that without His concurring aid we shall succeed in this political building no better than the builders of Babel."

> *The Divine strategy is the Christian... at his job day in and day out.*

We are now at a major turning point in our nation's history. Unprecedented prosperity continues to capture the headlines. Faster computers, wireless communication, high-speed access to the Internet—which has made the universe a global village—and all manner of technological wizardry is transforming our lives. Progress is what this nation is all about—Harvey and I were part of it—but in the center of this explosive growth and personal development, we must also ask, *What does it profit a person if he gains the whole world and lose his own soul?* Dr. Richard C. Halverson, a valued friend and colleague of both Harvey and me for so many years, sums up the strong medicine we need to counter our wild quest for fast fortune and instant fame. He writes,

> *The Divine strategy is the Christian . . . at his job day in and day out, bearing witness to Christ by life and lip right where he lives and works. In business and industry, the government and professions, labor, education, the military . . . in strategic places around the world. . . . This spiritual penetration is the clue to the incredible, incalculable impact of Christianity worldwide! The Christian teacher doing his job to the glory of God, not preaching, just living Christ around the clock, honoring Christ in his daily walk and talk. The student witnessing for Christ on the campus: in the fraternity house or dormitory or on the football field, in the student lounge. The Christian labor leader, businessman, military officer, policeman, surgeon, dentist, architect. . . . Multiply these by a million—by ten million—by a hundred million, and you have the true picture of Christian influence . . . invincible Christianity!* [2]

> **The Twelve learned by following and by living a life in which team-work proved essential.**

Although Dick Halverson penned those words more than 40 years ago, they remain the most viable of all

---

[2] Richard C. Halverson, *Between Sundays* (Grand Rapids, Mich.: Zondervan, 1965), p. 17.

Faithful pray-ers attend the monthly Breakfast Group meetings. They have been a profound reminder to me of the importance of working together in ministry.

solutions available to the challenges of the times in which we live. To meet the spiritual needs of our nation and our people, however, we dare not go it alone.

Over the years, my affiliation with the prayer breakfast movement and International Christian Leadership has been a profound reminder to me of the importance of working together in ministry. In the ICL *Breakfast, Luncheon and Fireside Groups Handbook,* there is a page I have referred to for many years that speaks to the importance of working together in ministry. In summary it says we must remember that when Jesus brought together that first handful of friends, Andrew, Peter, James, and John, He showed them a way of life in which everything depended upon close, intimate human relationships. The disciples met as a band of men, not because they belonged to an organization, but because they belonged to Jesus and to each other. This "family" quality was the core of their discipleship. The Twelve learned by following and by living a life in which teamwork proved essential.

What about today? Why is such accountability still vital for our spiritual survival as we enter a new millennium? I would suggest these reasons:

• To provide fellowship, so that we may share corporate spiritual experience with those of different backgrounds, without regard to creeds, orders, sacraments, and historic practices, and so that we may achieve the teamwork and united strength needed in today's world.

• To provide an opportunity for spiritual and moral development, thus influencing homes, industry, church, and government.

• To provide an opportunity for the practice of prayer and Bible study.

• To demonstrate the abundant life and power that Christ makes possible, opening up to increasingly greater numbers the possibilities and the desirability of the better way of life.

Faith to Make It When Times Are Tough

On a cold cellar wall in Cologne, Germany, an unknown World War II fugitive who was running from the Nazis left a lasting testimony of his faith. Workers one day found the inscription while clearing away the debris from the bombed-out house. It read,

I believe in the sun
Even when it is not shining.
I believe in love
Even when I do not feel it.
I believe in God
Even when He is silent.

At the close of chapter one I quoted Arnold Glasgow, who wrote, "Don't part company with your ideals. They are anchors in a time of storm." Such a statement is worth hearing repeatedly. During the storms and stress of business reversals, relationship challenges, and

> *"The power of God is released when the believer begins to praise."*

adversity of every kind—all of which are sure to come in a person's life—we may be tempted to lose our bearings, compromise our integrity, depart from the faith of our childhood, and forsake what is right and honorable in the sight of God. This short-term thinking will never serve us well. Fortunately, there is an answer to this spiritual and ethical dilemma, and it is found in the great apostle's letter to the Philippians (4:6), where Paul provides three guidelines for Christians who face insurmountable difficulty. He encourages us by saying:

1. *Be anxious for nothing.* He declares that worry is fruitless when we can trust in the wisdom of our Heavenly Father. When the call to battle was sounded for the volunteer army of the great Garibaldi, the soldiers responded, "Where are we going?" The officers replied, "That is a mystery, but our leader knows, and that's enough!"

2. *Be thankful for anything.* Tight corners give us an opportunity to be grateful for all that is available through our Heavenly Father's rich supply. Dr. Charles Stanley has said, "The power of God is released when the believer begins to praise, for this says to the Lord, 'I approve of what You are doing and am relying on Your strength.'"

3. *Be prayerful about everything.* God may allow us to get into a predicament so that we will diligently seek His face and wait upon Him. A hymn writer expressed it this way: "How oft in the conflict, when pressed by the foe, I have fled to my Refuge and breathed out my woe."

Although it is now considered ancient history by some, I still remember how during the Great Depression the entire nation breathed out its woe. If there were ever a time for a deep, abiding faith in the mercy of almighty God, that was the hour. We saw quick declines in the production and sale of goods and a sudden, severe rise in the ranks of the unemployed. Harvey and I discovered from painful personal experience that businesses and banks could close their doors overnight. People everywhere lost their jobs, their homes, and their livelihood. At one time as many as 15 million Americans—one-quarter of the

> **Will you be willing to stand alone— against the crowd...**

nation's workforce—were unemployed. Only those with an unshakable faith in God and themselves, and who held a belief that our nation could pull out of the crisis, survived—and thrived.

The writer to the Hebrews was my source of comfort then, just as he is ready to encourage us as we enter a new millennium, when he writes, "So do not throw away your confidence; it will be richly rewarded. You need to persevere so that when you have done the will of God, you will receive what he has promised" (Hebrews 10:35–36, NIV). Will your road ahead be a journey of faith when things get rough? Will you be willing to stand alone—against the crowd—and believe that there is great, unlimited potential in the *faith and power of one individual?* Rosa Parks had such faith—and her confidence changed segregation laws throughout the South because she had the temerity to sit in the front of a public bus. Ralph Nader had such faith—and from his unwavering commitment to the average citizen came the consumer protection movement, which he started in his 20s. Today, Nader's efforts have saved literally thousands of lives and prevented millions of injuries. Rachel Carson had such faith—and her landmark book *Silent Spring* activated the environmental movement that continues today, again proof positive of the power of one person who says, *It can be done, and I will do it!*

> **It can be done, and I will do it!**

It is my prayer that you will be a person of such faith, optimism, and vision as you travel the road ahead of you.

Wisdom for the Journey

As we come to the end of this book and my story, I want to leave you with some of the wisdom of the men and women who have inspired me in my work and ministry over the years. I have not always heeded their advice, but I have always known where to go to get it when I needed it. Perhaps among the following quotes you will find strength for a weary spirit and confidence that, with God as your helper, you, too, will find the inner resolve, the power, and the drive to be all God created you to be.

The greatest tragedy in life is people who have sight but no vision.
Helen Keller

Even if it's a little thing, do something for those who have a need of help, something for which you get no pay but the privilege of doing it.
Dr. Albert Schweitzer

Success is not getting to the top—but how you bounce on the bottom that counts.
George Patton

Unlike other resources, time cannot be bought or sold, borrowed or stolen, stocked up or saved, manufactured, reproduced, or modified. All we can do is to make use of it. And whether we use it or not, it nevertheless slips away.
Jean-Louis Servan-Schreiber

Be curious always! For knowledge will not acquire you; you must acquire it.
Sudie Back

Show class, have pride, and display character. If you do, winning takes care of itself.
Paul "Bear" Bryant

Heart is what separates the good from the great.
Michael Jordan

We enjoy warmth because we have been cold. We appreciate light because we have been in darkness. By the same token, we can experience joy because we have known sorrow.
David L. Weatherford

I close this series of quotes with a passage of Scripture on which I have built my life, my work at Fidelity Engineering Corporation, my present, and my eternal future. I referred to these words earlier, but they cannot be repeated enough.

Blessed is the man
  who does not walk in the counsel of the wicked
or stand in the way of sinners
  or sit in the seat of mockers.
But his delight is in the law of the LORD,
  and on his law he meditates day and night.
He is like a tree planted by streams of water,
  which yields its fruit in season
and whose leaf does not wither.
  Whatever he does prospers.

Not so the wicked!
  They are like chaff
  that the wind blows away.
Therefore the wicked will not stand in the judgment,
  nor sinners in the assembly of the righteous.
For the LORD watches over the way of the righteous,
  but the way of the wicked will perish.

It is now my privilege to share with you my spiritual Last Will and Testament. It is simple and to the point, does not need to be divided, and must be shared equally with all. I give you . . .

My abiding faith in the Person of Jesus Christ, Savior and Lord. Through Jesus alone can our sins be forgiven and our future assured. I believe this with all my heart, and I share this good news with you.

My optimism for our nation. We will continue to be hit by forces of evil from within and without, just as we have been challenged in the past. However, I am confident as people of faith, strong morals, and extraordinary good will stand up for what is right, that our country will continue to be a positive force in a world of so much darkness.

My belief in today's youth—but only as our young people pursue the wisdom and counsel of Psalm 1 that promises whatever he—or she—does prospers. This assurance comes with the condition that they must be planted by streams of waters.

My commitment to being a servant of God and a friend to all until the Lord takes me to be with Him. The name I chose for our young company so many years ago was Fidelity—a name it continues to bear today—which comes from the Latin word for "faithfulness." I trust that in the final analysis, our company and its dedicated employees will be judged worthy of its name.

What is your legacy? What do you plan to write in your own spiritual Last Will and Testament? Will you leave a host of healthy relationships behind, people who so love and admire you that you will be truly missed? What will you be known for? What have you believed and passionately fought for in your life? Will our world be a better place because you showed up, did your work, and lived a life of honor to God? I hope so. The good news is that you still have time to invest heavily in those relationships that can make your life a trophy to God's grace. With that challenge, I leave you with these questions and thoughts:

Is someone happier because you passed his way today?

Did you bring a smile to a clouded face when you did not turn away?

Is someone's burden lighter for just a little lift, a pleasant word, a little boost, or perhaps some little gift?

Do you feel content and happy when you settle down at night because you found a troubled friend and help to set him right?

A load is always lighter when a friend walks by your side. You cannot cure all ills, but at least you know you tried.

Let not one single day go by at home, at work, at play . . . unless someone is happier because you passed his way.

God bless you and keep you.

Your friend,

Clarence W. Hottel

P.S. Today is a dentist appointment. When I arrive, the nurse leads me to the room, and while I am getting into my chair my friend, Dr. Keith Schmidt, comes in with his usual smile and sense of humor, and asks, "How are you today? Are you keeping on the straight and narrow?" My answer is, "I'm trying." Later I thought about that. It is a good question for anyone to think about, because the alternate route is the wide, crowded, fast road to destruction. Actually, we don't have much choice if we want to be sure of our success—as promised in Psalm 1. Whatsoever he doeth will prosper is a reward that is eternal.